Rita,

A BOAT SPENDS 95% OF IT'S LIFE AT ANCHOR. DON'T L YOUR LIFE LIKE THAT.

LOVE HARD / PADDLE HARDER

LOVE, Michael

9/29/23

ESCAPING THE VELVET RUT

AN ADVENTURER'S GUIDE TO CHASING YOUR DREAMS

By Michael Schnitzka

www.TheVelvetRut.com

Editor: Julie Kastello
Copy Editor: Kristine Krueger
Page Design: Sue Myers
Cover Design and Map Illustrations: Teri Gehin
Brand Development: Kirsten Jaeckle
Author Photograph: WineGuyPhotography.com

ISBN 978-1-9812-7998-2

Dedicated to my canoeing partner, Bill Perdzock.

With special thanks to my favorite support crew,
Mike Mlynarski and Rod Hanson,
along with my other support crews, friends,
family and sponsors.

Without your help, I could never have
chased so many dreams.

TABLE OF CONTENTS

INTRODUCTION

The "velvet rut." An intriguing term, isn't it? I've heard different definitions for it over the years. But it most often refers to a job that is no longer challenging or fulfilling, but is difficult to leave because it offers great pay, good benefits and plenty of perks.

But the term doesn't have to refer to employment. It can refer to anything—your marriage, the place you live, even the car you drive—that you continue to endure in your life even though it doesn't make you happy. In fact, getting stuck in a velvet rut in any area of your life can prevent you from achieving your dreams and making the most out of every moment.

People get stuck in a velvet rut, because, as the word *velvet* suggests, it's soft, luxurious, *comfortable*. When you're in a velvet rut, you're going through the motions, coasting along, not actively participating. You may be bored, or worse, gritting your teeth to make it through the day. But you won't quit. Why? Because change is hard. Because you fear the unknown. Because you might not find a job with such a lucrative salary or so many vacation days. Because it's easier to go to work every day than upset the status quo.

The velvet rut is comfortable, but it sucks. It keeps people from pursuing their goals. It keeps them from making the most out of every moment. It slowly anesthetizes them until they forget the adventures they planned to take, the exotic places they wanted to visit, the dreams they wanted to chase.

For many people, it takes a dramatic event like a job termination or health crisis to drive them from their velvet rut. I've heard people say the day they got fired is one of the best days of their life, because it forced them out of a job that they never would've left on their own. It might take years, but they look back and say, "Getting fired is the best thing that ever happened!" Because otherwise, they would still be sitting in that office every day, grinding their teeth and staring at the walls.

Now, I'm not advising you to get fired from your job. I'm suggesting you take a good, hard look at your life to identify areas where you're stuck in a velvet rut. Take time to figure out what you want out of life and what makes you happy. Find the courage to make the necessary changes. Then pursue your dreams and live a life without regret.

CHAPTER 1

HOTTER
THAN HADES

"Sweat is just fat crying."
~*Source unknown*

June 21, 2015

The sun broke over the Buckskin mountain range several hours ago, causing the temperature on the floor of the desert to jump from 80° to 110° in just a few minutes. Now, it's about 11:30 a.m. and even hotter. I feel like I stepped into a 500° oven as I pedal my bicycle north on State Road 95 toward Parker, Arizona.

Our two-man team is on the second day of the 3,000-mile Race Across America, and the heat has been a killer since we left Oceanside, California, north of San Diego. My partner, Dave Traxel, and I began by taking turns trying to bicycle 30-minute periods in this nonstop bike race. But the scorching temperatures hit Dave hard, so he cut short several of his shifts. Not wanting to lose ground, I picked up the slack by increasing the length of mine. Dave's condition continued to go downhill throughout the first day, and we couldn't determine if it was cramping, dehydration or something else. So Dave spent more time resting in the air-conditioned support van than biking. During the night, when the temperature dropped a bit, he seemed to bounce back and was biking faster and finishing his shifts.

But this morning, Dave is struggling again and unable to pull his weight. I know the oppressive heat is taking a toll on him; it's doing the same to me. Two members of our support crew—Dave Allen and Ellen Holly—have been in the van with him, doing all they can to get him back into racing condition while I bike. So far, nothing has done the trick.

Lack of sleep, extra time in the saddle and the unbearable heat have shortened my temper. Frustrated with Dave's inability to bike for very long, I told my crew to try something else, because I needed Dave to kick it up a notch—and soon.

Up until moments ago, I'd been resting in the support van, which followed right behind Dave as he biked. But when he signaled that he needed a rest, we decided it would be best if Dave Allen and Ellen left me behind to continue biking while they drove my partner 7 miles ahead to Time Station No. 4 on the race route where the remaining three members of our crew waited in our RV. I'm hoping a change of atmosphere or a cold shower in the RV will revive him, because I'm exhausted and can't continue much longer without a few hours of sleep.

I refill my two water bottles from the cooler in the support van before it drives off. Then I clip my shoes into my pedals and follow down the highway on my bike.

I watch as the white van becomes a speck in the distance, and then I hear a *pffft*. Damn! A sharp stone in the road popped my back tire, and it's flat. Seriously? Now what?

I'm out in the desert by myself. I don't have a spare tire. I don't have a cell phone. I don't have anything. The support van that was always behind me if I needed assistance is gone.

All the other teams are ahead of us, and we're in dead-last place. It's just me. And the sagebrush. And the unrelenting sun beating down on the shimmering-hot asphalt as it crosses the flat terrain. There are no towns, no cars and no shade in sight. In that one minute, I go through the list of options in my mind, and what I come up with is this: *you're screwed.*

◆

I unclip my cycling shoes from the bike pedals. The cleats on the bottom make it difficult to walk on the road, so I briefly consider taking off my shoes.

But I know I can't walk barefoot on 130° pavement. All I can think is that my crew will be waiting for me *there*. So I start pushing my bike as I walk toward our meeting spot 7 miles away. *Clip-clop, clip-clop, clip-clop.*

On the bike, I could probably get there in 20 minutes. On foot, at this pace, it's going to take much longer to reach them, maybe 2 hours or more. I'm hoping the crew notices that I'm behind schedule and drives back to find out why. *Clip-clop, clip-clop.*

It's Hades-hot out here. I'm wearing a white, long-sleeve sunscreen shirt and white cycling shorts, but still baking under the sun's harsh rays. It's so bright, I'd be blinded without my mirrored sunglasses. I remove my sweat-soaked gloves and flex my fingers. I take off my bike helmet, and the cotton skull cap I'm wearing beneath it is drenched with sweat, so I remove that too. Aah, that feels good...for a minute. Then I feel the sun searing the top of my head, so I put the helmet back on. Rivulets of sweat trickle down my face and back. Have you ever opened an oven door and felt prickly as the heat hits you? That's how my whole body feels—like it's on pins and needles. I think you could light a match just by holding it next to me. *Clip-clop, clip-clop.*

RED-HOT RACE. Michael Schnitzka bikes Arizona's State Road 95 on the smoldering second day of the Race Across America.

The drinking water in my bottles is now the same as the air temperature, about 120°. That's steamier than a hot tub. Should I drink it? I don't want to, but I need to stay hydrated. My mouth is so dry that all I can think of is how good cool, refreshing water will feel running down my throat. I take a gulp from my bottle, and it's like swallowing the hottest soup you can imagine. Ugh. I go on. *Clip-clop, clip-clop.*

Way down the road I see movement. It looks white. What is it? Is it the support van heading my way? That's gotta be it. Who else would be out here? *Clip-clop, clip-clop.*

I squint my eyes, focusing on the spot, which undulates in the heat. Crap, that's not the van. The white dot is a small bush at a bend in the road, and the rippling movement is a mirage caused by the heat. I really thought it was the van. My mind is playing tricks on me. *Clip-clop, clip-clop.*

Thoughts chase through my brain, one after another, as I sift through my options, explore possibilities, search for alternatives. Then a question pops into my head and lingers. *Why am I here?* I'd trained for 2 years and spent $5,000—including the entrance fee, gas, RV rental, food and much more—to be here. And I remind myself, *Oh, that's right—I'm paying to do this! I want to do this.* So I keep walking, walking, walking… *Clip-clop, clip-clop, clip-clop.*

A beat-up old Ford pickup truck drives up from behind and stops. Two Hispanic men jump out. They start talking, but I don't speak Spanish, so I can't understand what they're saying. They obviously think I'm in trouble. Why else would a sane person be walking a bike out in the middle of nowhere in this heat?

They reach for my bicycle to put it in the back of their truck, so they can take me to the next town. But I almost have to push them away, because I can't explain that if I go with them, that means I quit the race. And I'm definitely not quitting this race. They finally give up, shake their heads and look at me like, "You're a dumb ass!" Then they get in their truck and leave. I imagine as they pull away, they're looking in the rearview mirror and saying, "That guy is going to be dead in an hour." *Clip-clop, clip-clop.*

My overheated brain estimates the distance I've walked, and I think I'm about 4 miles into my 7-mile trek to catch up with my support crew.

I can't remember ever being this thirsty. My tongue feels like it's stuck to the roof of my mouth. I don't have much water left, but I decide to finish it. The steamy liquid is so disgusting I can barely gag it down. I've been in more than my fair share of sucky situations, but this one has to be the suckiest of them all.

I paddled a canoe for 62 hours without sleep when setting a record time on the Wisconsin River. I survived flipping a canoe in the icy waters of the Rhine River in Europe not once, but three times. I kept up with Navy SEALs running up, down and across Rib Mountain in Wisconsin while training nonstop for 34 hours. Out of all the brutal moments I've faced during my adventures, drinking friggin' hot water when it's 120° outside is by far the worst.

It's only Day 2 of the RAAM, and it's living up to its name as the world's toughest bike race. And there are still 2,700 miles of pedaling to go before we cross the country and reach the end of the race in Annapolis, Maryland.

Clip-clop, clip-clop, clip-clop.

CHAPTER 2

THOSE CRAZY, LAZY, HAZY DAYS OF SUMMER

*"The best time to plant a tree was
20 years ago. The second best time is now."*
~Chinese proverb

I have been a pallbearer 13 times. At the funeral home, as I looked down on these individuals in their caskets, I wondered if they got out of life everything they wanted. If they were given just one more day to live, what would they do?

If I could, I'd ask, "Were you happy with your life? Did you accomplish what you wanted?" I'm curious what they would say. I think a lot of people would probably reply, "No, I'm not done. I didn't get to do half the things I wanted. All I did was work."

My mother died slowly of brain cancer in 1993 at age 56. I remember being at the hospital with my sister when my father asked the doctor, "Is this something I need to worry about for my kids?" The doctor assured my dad this type of cancer wasn't hereditary.

Six years later, my mother's sister's son—a cousin on my mom's side—was diagnosed with the same type of brain cancer and died at 40. Not hereditary? I think about that often: My cousin was 40 and done. Those two events have been a big driving force in my life, pushing me to make the most of every moment.

Come my last day on Earth, if someone asks me, "Did you accomplish everything you wanted?" I want to be able to say, "Yes, I'm good. I can go now."

What about you? If you were told you had a year, a month, a week or even a day to live, would you regret not finding the time for the things you hoped to do? Or would you spend that remaining time achieving as many of your dreams as possible?

This life we are given is not a dress rehearsal. This is all you get. **Tomorrow is promised to no one.**

———◆———

My father, Richard, and my mother, Sharon, raised our family in the village of Menomonee Falls on the northwest side of Milwaukee, Wisconsin. My dad ran his own insurance brokerage firm, and my mom was a homemaker. My sister, Sheryl, and I had a typical, happy upbringing in the suburbs.

In my junior year of high school, I was on the track team with Bill Perdzock, also a junior. He and I didn't have many classes together, but we soon became good friends.

SIGN ME UP. Michael Schnitzka stands by the state historical marker that inspired his canoe trip down the Wisconsin River with Bill Perdzock.

A couple of years later, in the fall of 1982, Bill invited me up to his family's cabin in northern Wisconsin to go deer hunting. Opening day of gun season— November 20—was fairly warm with temperatures in the lower 40s, and it was raining like crazy. The conditions were terrible for hunting. Heck, the conditions were terrible for deer. They bed down in weather like that and don't want to come out to play.

Because the cabin didn't have a TV or radio, Bill and I decided to head into town to hit some bars and kill a little time. We drank a few beers at a local tavern, then decided it would be cheaper to buy a case of beer from the liquor store. We picked up the beer and stopped at a wayside rest area between Land O' Lakes and Conover to listen to the car radio.

From our parking spot, we could read a state historical marker about the Wisconsin River. The marker notes that the river starts nearby, travels nearly the entire length of the state and empties into the Mississippi just below Prairie du Chien. That's a total of 300 miles. In the condition we were in—which I admit was a bit inebriated—I said, "Bill, we should travel the entire thing like Huck Finn did!" He shook his head "no" and cracked open another beer.

Over the course of the weekend, I kept bringing up the idea to Bill. I wasn't going to take "no" for an answer. As a last resort, I basically double-dog-dared Bill to join me. Only then did he finally agree to embark on our canoeing adventure. Little did we know at the time that the state marker was way off on the length of the Wisconsin River. It must have been measured as the crow flies. The real length when paddling the river is 430 miles.

———◆———

Once back home, we started the wheels in motion to accomplish our trip. Bill and I were both in college at the time, so we couldn't start our trip until summer vacation. But that gave us plenty of time to prepare. This was a lesson we learned early on: If you plan for the worst and it happens, you will be prepared.

First things first: We needed a canoe. Bill's family owned a stock aluminum model that was super-heavy and built like a battleship, so we agreed it would be our vessel.

Back then, technology was much more limited and we couldn't jump on the Internet to surf the Web for information about canoeing the Wisconsin River. We went to the local library to do our research. We soon found out the library didn't have the detailed river maps we wanted. Our next-best option was a standard state map—the kind for sale at most gas stations.

During our research at the library, we came across photos showing canoes equipped with covers to keep out the wind and waves. Bill's mother—I always address her as Mrs. P.—was a seamstress and had a very good sewing machine at home. We commissioned her to design and sew a cover for the canoe. She was enthusiastic about our trip and happy to help us. She took us to a fabric store, where we purchased yards of ripstop nylon—a very light and durable material that would be perfect for the cover.

Mrs. P. sewed the cover and reinforced the edges with batting to make it stronger. Then she left it up to us to figure out how to attach it to the canoe.

You might think Bill and I would have appreciated more help. But that's not how we like to work. Half the fun in doing anything is noodling out how to do it. I'm not exaggerating when I say that Bill can do everything—electrical, woodworking, mechanical. Give him a bucket of nuts and bolts, and he can build a car. He's that talented.

As far as personalities go, Bill and I are like *The Odd Couple*. I'm Oscar. He's Felix. I'm loud and wear my emotions on my sleeve. Bill is quiet, focused and determined. Although we seem like opposites, we work very well together.

To attach the cover to canoe, Bill drilled holes in the aluminum every 5 or 6 inches along the top edge of the canoe. Then, one by one, he riveted a "male" half of a snap to the canoe where he had drilled each hole.

While he did that, I sat nearby working on the cover. I punched holes along the thick edge of the fabric to match the ones Bill had drilled in the canoe. Then, a section at a time, I placed the edge of the cover on a small block of wood. I used a hammer to tap together the two parts of the "female" half of a snap where I'd punched each hole.

When we were done, the cover easily snapped onto the canoe. We could pull it until it was almost skintight. Mrs. P. had designed the cover to have spray skirts like a kayak. The skirts had rope around the perimeter, so they could be cinched around our waists to keep out the rain. If it rained, the water would run down our jackets over the skirts and back into the river.

We would need a lot of gear for our trip, so Bill built a big wooden box with metal handles to store it. The idea was if the canoe flipped, the box would float and keep all of our supplies together and dry. Bill went all out on the construction of the box, finishing it and shellacking it to a shine. It was so sturdy you could drive a truck over it. He even equipped it with a rubber seal around the lid to keep out water. That kind of attention to detail would serve us well in later adventures.

—◆—

Not having embarked on a trip like this before, Bill and I packed pretty much everything we could imagine we might need. There were the necessities: a pup tent, sleeping bags, fishing rods, clothing and food. Bill attached chains to an old metal camera tripod to hold a grill grate, so we could cook meals over a campfire. Into the wooden storage box went loaves of cheap white bread, peanut butter and jelly, canned soup and other canned goods. And we added a small kerosene lantern and container of kerosene. Unfortunately, we'd soon discover that after a few days in the box, all our food tasted like kerosene. And we'd quickly learn that we went overboard on the fishing gear, lures, tackle boxes and extra camping gear.

On May 31, 1983, we loaded up Bill's blue 1968 Pontiac Tempest with our supplies and strapped the canoe to its roof. We drove up to his family's cabin, stayed the night and set out on our adventure the next morning.

The actual start of the Wisconsin River is at a dam where the water leaves Lac Vieux Desert, near the border of the Upper Peninsula of Michigan. That dam conveniently happens to be located about a mile from Bill's cabin.

We drove to the dam, unstrapped the canoe and emptied out Bill's car. Bill drove his car to the cabin, parked it, then walked back the mile to the dam. We put the canoe in the river and just started paddling.

The river starts in a wild area in northern Wisconsin with very few cabins and amazing scenery. It was June, so all the trees were lush with leaves. The river is fairly narrow here, so in places, tree branches from both sides met over our heads, totally shading the river. It was like canoeing through a beautiful green tunnel.

When I say the area was "wild," I mean that as we'd come around a bend in the river, we wouldn't be surprised to encounter anything. There were all kinds of birds—herons, cranes, ducks, hawks and so many other species. We saw lots of wildlife—white-tailed deer, raccoons, turtles and even a few otters.

We often paddled by beavers swimming in the river. When they get frightened, they take their tails and smack the water. It's so loud it sounds like a gun going off! A few times, we didn't know beavers were nearby until we heard the loud *thwack* as their tails smacked the water. On a peaceful evening, that sound would make us

MISSISSIPPI OR BUST! Michael Schnitzka (left) and Bill Perdzock strike a pose before embarking on their 1983 Huck Finn canoe adventure down the Wisconsin River.

just about jump out of our seats!

Because we weren't in a hurry, we leisurely paddled, enjoying the scenery. As it got close to dark, we picked a spot on the shore to make our first camp. We set up a small pup tent—just big enough for the two of us to squeeze into with our sleeping bags. We started a campfire and warmed up a few cans of soup we'd packed in the wooden box Bill had built. Then we settled in, got comfortable and relaxed until we decided to go to bed.

There was a casual routine to our days, yet every day was different. We had no timeline. Some days, we got up at 10 a.m., ate oatmeal for breakfast and then hopped in the canoe. We coasted, just drifting along until 3 p.m. when we found a sandy bank to set up camp.

Other days, when the river had a good current, we said, "Let's put on some miles." We paddled until 6 or 7 at night. It wasn't unusual for us to catch a few northern pike or smallmouth bass while we paddled, then we cooked the fish over our campfire at night.

————◆————

The Wisconsin River is called the nation's hardest-working river, because it has 26 hydroelectric dams that produce electricity along its 430 miles. In actuality, there are 26 dams in *330 miles*, because the last 100 miles of the

FOOTLOOSE AND FANCY-FREE. Michael Schnitzka takes a leisurely break as Bill Perdzock snaps this photo during their Wisconsin River canoe trip.

river flows freely to the Mississippi River.

Dams are marked to alert boaters and canoeists of upcoming portages. Signs mark the location where watercraft should be taken out of the river above the dam as well as the location where it's safe to put in the craft below the dam.

Bill and I realized on our first portage that we had packed far too much equipment. We each had to make four trips to get the canoe and all our gear around the dam. With many more portages ahead of us, we realized we were going to spend a lot of time transporting our supplies by foot.

To minimize the distance we had to carry all of our equipment, we started to cheat a little on each portage to get as close to the dam as possible. The portage at the Otter Rapids Dam west of Eagle River ended up being the scariest one on our trip. Instead of putting the canoe back in the water where it was marked, about 100 yards down from the dam, we decided to put in right below the dam. This turned out to be a bad idea.

Two 4-foot circular pipes jutted out of the dam, pouring water back into the river. We didn't realize the water that came out circled back around, creating an eddy. When Bill and I pushed off from shore to start paddling, the swirling current pulled us back very close to those pipes. The roaring water was so loud Bill and I could hardly hear each other shout as we tried to figure out what to do. We ended up clinging to a nearby wall of moss-covered bricks. The slippery surface made it difficult for us to hold on and stay in one place.

WISCONSIN RIVER

LAC VIEUX DESERT

WAUSAU

STEVENS POINT

WISCONSIN DELLS

PRAIRIE DU CHIEN

THE 430-MILE WISCONSIN RIVER literally cuts the state in half.

Eventually, we couldn't hang on anymore and used our canoe paddles to push off hard from the wall, hoping this would send our canoe into the current. Luckily, we shot past the big wall of water and down the river, wiser and no worse for the experience.

———◆———

In the middle of the state is the Petenwell Flowage, which is 25 miles long and 5 miles across, making it the second largest inland lake in the state. The lake is so long that when you enter it, because of the curvature of the earth, you can't see the other end of the lake. This was going to be our biggest test of open water, which can be very dangerous if it's windy. We were lucky there was no wind, and we chose to camp on an island near the west shore. As we set up camp, a thunderstorm began to slide by us to the south. The rain and wind didn't reach us, but we had front-row seats to a fantastic show of lightning as we ate our dinner next to the campfire.

There are some experiences that are seared into your memory because they're so cool. This was one of them. It wasn't dark yet. The sun was starting to set, and it gave an orange-pinkish cast to the clouds. Then these massive lightning bolts intermittently lit up the sky. It was really neat. Bill had brought a tape recorder and cassettes on our trip, so we could listen to music. He'd also packed a blank cassette, so we used it to record ourselves describing the lightning show. Listening to the tape now really brings back the wonder and awe of that evening.

A few days later, we entered the Wisconsin Dells. Now, keep in mind it was mid-June in a popular resort area, so everyone was out on the water. Besides all the vacationers boating and canoeing, there were big tourist boats giving group excursions of the remarkable rock formations and towering sandstone cliffs the area is known for.

A section of the river called "The Narrows" is banked by tall rock cliffs and

A HEAVY BURDEN. Bill Perdzock looks over all the equipment and supplies he and Michael Schnitzka carried when they portaged around a dam on their trip.

BACKSEAT DRIVER. Bill Perdzock takes this photo of Michael Schnitzka paddling their canoe as they enter "The Narrows" in scenic Wisconsin Dells.

provides a narrow passageway. This part of the river was especially difficult for us to navigate. As the big tourist boats cruised past, they made big waves in an area where there was little room to share. The 50-foot rock walls don't dissipate waves like a sloping shoreline does. Instead, the water hit the walls and bounced back, creating erratic waves that made it hard to balance in a canoe. It felt like we were going to flip any second.

Despite some treacherous moments, the Dells offered us one of our coolest campsites. We discovered a sandy spot under a sandstone cliff overhang that was only accessible from the river. We pulled the canoe on shore and left our supplies inside. The outcropping was just big enough to fit our tent underneath, so we wouldn't have to worry if it rained. It was almost like being in a cave, and we wondered who had slept in this same spot a hundred—or even a thousand—years ago. We woke up the next morning to find several boats with fishermen within yards of our campsite. We quietly packed up our gear and slipped into the water.

The next "big" city on our map was Portage—so named because explorers used it as a portage from the Wisconsin River on one side of the city to the Fox River on the other side. The Wisconsin River flows south and the Fox River a mile away flows north. So travelers could paddle from northern Wisconsin down to the city of Portage, walk a mile to get to the Fox River, and then paddle north all the way to Green Bay.

Before we left on our trip, we had made plans with some college buddies back home to meet in Portage, because it was the closest city to Milwaukee. A few days before we expected to reach Portage, we made a collect call and set up a meeting spot at a specific bridge. We adjusted our paddling the next day or two, so we had plenty of time to set up camp on a large island in the river near our meeting spot.

It was great to see that big station wagon pull up and a half-dozen of our friends spill out of the doors. Bill and I shuttled back and forth many times to take our friends and their camping equipment out to the island. We made a big campfire on a sandbar, cooked dinner, drank beer and swapped stories all night.

Not long after the city of Portage is the last dam at Prairie du Sac. From this point on, the Wisconsin River flows freely and runs through wild areas with tall bluffs, dense forests and open marshes. After a few days of paddling, we calculated the day we expected to arrive in Bridgeport—the end of our trip. We stopped in Muscoda, and I called my parents to set up the time and date to pick us up.

———◆———

I felt sad those final days before the finish, knowing this adventure would soon come to an end. This trip was the first time I had enjoyed complete independence. No rules. No regulations. No parents. No school. Just doing

SHELTERED SITE. Bill Perdzock begins to set up camp beneath a rock outcropping in Wisconsin Dells. The campsite is protected from rain and only inches from the water.

whatever I wanted whenever I wanted.

I knew I was going to miss the times of us drifting along in the canoe, just talking. Bill and I discussed all kinds of topics: our families, sports, girls, college, jobs and our dreams for the future.

Already at that point, I was feeling that I didn't want to get married until I was 30, no matter who I met. I figured if I got married at 30, that would give me at least 30 years with that person. So taking the 10 or 12 years until then for myself was fair. It was my time to get to know me.

I think it's important that people *make* time to get to know who they really are inside. And I said *make* time, not *take* time, because it won't happen unless you set aside a specific time to think about who you are and what you want in life.

Life gets busy. You have work, children and routine responsibilities like paying bills, shopping for groceries and doing the laundry. I understand that you can't skip those things. But carve out time for yourself, whether it's 5 minutes at the end of the day, a couple of hours one Saturday a month or a single day of your hard-earned vacation. Heck, use the time while you're mowing the lawn or commuting to work to think about what makes you happy and what dreams you want to pursue.

And don't think this is something you only need to do once or something you only do when you're young. People change as they acquire new experiences.

Make time to reassess your dreams and recognize when they no longer fit the person you've become. Because you can't make your dreams come true unless you know what they are.

———◆———

My parents were waiting for us as we paddled into Bridgeport. They couldn't believe how tan Bill and I were, but then again, we had been on the water for 18 days.

In the car on the way home, my mother handed me a newspaper article from the *Milwaukee Journal.* The story was about two men who had just set

CANOEING COMPADRES. Bill Perdzock and Michael Schnitzka shake hands at the base of the Bridgeport Bridge after completing their 18-day Wisconsin River adventure.

29

the record for speed, canoeing the Wisconsin River in 8 days, 3 hours and 13 minutes. I read the article. Then I read it again. I thought, *They passed us on the river. We were probably sleeping in that morning. They're paddling past us to make the record, and we're snoring in our little tent.*

"Eight days? That's not that good," I said. "We did it in 18 days, and we coasted most of the way."

Bill and I discussed it bit, then started to get analytical, calculating the speed we would have to go and the distance per day we would have to travel to beat the record.

"Let's go after this," I said to Bill.

"No," he replied.

"C'mon, Bill! Let's do it!" I said.

This is the point a tradition started. I double-dog-dared Bill to go after that speed record with me.

He jokingly replied, "If you can have somebody pay for all of it, I'll do it."

He would later learn to regret those words.

◆

Looking back on the 1983 paddle, I've come to realize the truth of the saying: "A journey of a thousand miles begins with a single step." This fun adventure of just enjoying life was my first step on a journey that would take me to so many different destinations in my life. I'm still amazed at the number of places I have visited and the number of amazing people I have met along the way.

These experiences allowed me to test every part of myself, both physically and mentally. It is the sum of the parts that make me up as a man.

CHAPTER 3

RESEARCH +
EXPERIENCE =
SUCCESS

*"Many of life's failures are people who did not realize
how close they were to success when they gave up."*
~Thomas Edison

O nly hours after completing our 18-day Wisconsin River canoe
adventure, I had challenged Bill to go after the speed record of
8 days, 3 hours that was set while we were out on the water.
When we got home, I immersed myself in the world of canoe
racing. I couldn't get information fast enough. I joined the
American Canoe Association, which included a subscription to *Canoe News*.
That magazine will play a role in a story to come.

My father is in sales, so I asked him how I should go about procuring a
racing canoe to pursue the record. He told me to go to the library and find
information on all the companies that make racing canoes. That list would be
the starting point.

The canoe company that was closest to Milwaukee was Wenonah Canoe
in Winona, Minnesota. My father and I discussed what I should say, which I
wrote down and eventually memorized. With my notes in front of me, I called

Mike Cichanowski, the president of Wenonah Canoe. "Hi, my name is Mike Schnitzka, and I would like to set a time record using your canoe," I said, as I started my pitch.

With no actual experience racing a canoe, I was hoping my youth and enthusiasm would help make my case. I did enough research on his company so he knew I was serious. I had picked out a few canoe models I thought would be good for the type of water we would encounter on the Wisconsin River. Not all canoes are made the same. Some are built for speed, but the design sacrifices space needed for gear. Some are great for turning in white water but are not suited for distance paddling.

The model I was really interested in was the Odyssey. It had a large bow to handle big waves, was long at 18 feet, 6 inches, and was built for speed. It was made of very lightweight Kevlar and cost $1,500. In 1983, this dollar amount to poor college kids was out of our financial ballpark. Because of the high cost, my father suggested I ask to simply borrow the canoe and give it back when we were done.

So I asked Mr. Cichanowski if he would lend us a racing canoe to go after the speed record paddling the Wisconsin River. He asked many questions about our previous experience, and I explained while we didn't have much, we had paddled the entire Wisconsin River, and we knew how to shave off time from the current speed record. Much to my amazement, he said, "Yes."

Bill and I eventually drove to Winona to pick up the Odyssey. Using a lightweight canoe was a key part of breaking the record. The aluminum canoe Bill and I had used for our Huck Finn adventure was a world away from this sleek, light, composite vessel. The more a canoe is shaped like a log with a round bottom (not flat like our aluminum canoe), the faster it will go. But that design also makes it more inclined to tip. If you think a big heavy aluminum canoe is tippy, try paddling a Kevlar racing canoe. If you are into NASCAR, you know the phrase "loose is fast." The same goes for canoes.

When Bill and I arrived, we met Mr. Cichanowski, who gave us a wonderful tour of his factory and showed us how his racing canoes were made. What made it official was the contract we signed to borrow the canoe. We promised if we had any media attention, we would mention his company name. Driving home, we couldn't believe we had this expensive boat strapped to the car and that we were committed to attempting the record after our college courses ended in May of the following year.

Bill and I knew we would have to improve everything we had done to be faster and more efficient. Mrs. P. also made a cover for this canoe to keep the wind, water and waves out of it. We purchased our very first bent-shaft racing paddles. Most paddles are straight from one end to the other. Racing paddles have a small bend in them just before the blade that goes in the water. It allows a longer paddling stroke before the blade starts lifting water. When you lift water up with your paddle, the opposite action happens in the canoe—your canoe dips a little. The name for that is "porpoising." When racing and paddling hard, the canoe should not look like it is bouncing up and down. It should look like you are sliding the canoe across ice on a lake, smooth and flat.

When we first traveled the Wisconsin River, we had noticed paddling at night during a full moon was not that difficult. We got out a calendar to determine when there would be a full moon to allow us to paddle at night safely. We also studied years of flood records to find out the best time to attempt the race—when the water was high but not dangerous.

This time, we finally found detailed maps of the river, so we could highlight the dangerous points and avoid them. We marked on each map the best place to portage, both in and out, to save time. Due to the large number of portages, we had to reduce the weight of all our equipment. Instead of packing heavy canned goods, we decided to take along high-quality dried foods.

We had a large collapsible plastic container to supply us with water, but we knew we couldn't finish the race without stopping a few times to refill it. We purchased the best athletic clothes we could afford at the time. We had polypropylene underwear and GORE-TEX rain shells to keep us both warm and dry.

DESIGN BY MOM. Bill Perdzock's mother, Mrs. P., uses newspaper to create a pattern for the spray skirt she's sewing for the canoe.

Bill and I worked on our paddling

technique until winter set in and the water froze. We joined a health club to get our bodies more muscular, so we could handle the pounding we were going to get paddling 430 miles as fast as possible. We learned some parts of the Milwaukee River don't freeze during the cold winter days, so occasionally we got in some real paddle time to keep our balance sharp. As soon as spring came, we were on the water getting boat time in when we weren't working.

◆

On June 8, 1984, Bill and I once again drove up to the start of the race by ourselves. We had a day to rest and get ready for the hardest thing we had ever done in our young lives. On June 10, with maps in hand and food and gear loaded in a huge daypack, we pushed off from the dam at Lac Vieux Desert in the Wenonah canoe. Our full moon would arrive 3 days later.

Needing to set a time record, we had to do a lot of night paddling. Bill was working for his father's company as an electrician, so he wired up the front of the canoe with a headlight that was powered by a small 12-volt motorcycle battery. We knew we would need to use the light sparingly, so Bill installed a foot switch that allowed him to turn it on and off as needed. We had tested it quite a bit before the race and learned we could get about 5 hours of light, so we only used it when we needed it.

LET THERE BE LIGHT. A motorcycle battery powers the canoe's headlight to allow paddling after dark.

Unlike the year before, this trip was all business. When we hit a portage, we made only one trip, not four. Comfortable campsites were not important. When it was time to sleep, we found a place on the shore to easily get out of and back into the water.

My job was to take the gear out of the canoe, set up the tent, roll out the sleeping bags and get everything ready so we could sleep. While I did that, Bill put together his small camping stove with a propane container. He boiled water to prepare some dried food to eat. We accomplished all that in an hour. Then we climbed into our sleeping bags to catch 3 hours of sleep. When our alarm went off, we reversed the process. I took down the camp, Bill cooked the food and then we hit the water.

As we had learned on our previous trip, the longest portage on the Wisconsin River is in Rhinelander, and it's almost a mile long. Due to the distance, the paper company in charge of the dam had a company pickup truck available to transport canoes and paddlers the length of the portage at no charge. Because we were trying to set a time record, we felt taking advantage of a free ride would be cheating, so we carried our canoe and gear instead.

One area that worried us, of course, was the Wisconsin Dells, which had been difficult to navigate on our previous trip due to the large number of tourism boats and vacationers on the water. But we hit that area midweek and at night, so there was virtually no boat traffic.

The area that gave us new problems was past the last dam in Prairie du Sac. The Wisconsin River flows freely the last 100 miles, and there are thousands of sandbars that come and go over time as the current moves the sand around. This means the main river channel can change from year to year. While paddling in the dark the last two nights, Bill and I struggled because we kept running into sandbars that had not been there the year before. While the moon's light makes it easier to see things ahead of you, it does not illuminate what's below the surface of the water.

FAST FOOD. Bill Perdzock eats a quick meal at a campsite on shore before crawling into his sleeping bag for his nightly 3 hours of sleep.

I've mentioned that a race like this takes an incredible amount of planning and preparation. But put that thought aside for a minute and let me tell you about the race itself. Once you get the paddle in your hands and start pulling on it, canoeing is the most difficult sport you can imagine. During a triathlon, you get breaks, meaning you use your arms and shoulders when you're swimming, but then you get on a bike, and your legs work while your arms and shoulders rest.

That doesn't happen when you're paddling. It's your shoulders, your arms, your core, your back, your everything—grinding, grinding, grinding. It's like feeling you're going uphill on a bicycle, and it's never-ending. The only time you get to *not* pull on that paddle is when you're eating or sleeping. Otherwise, you're pulling, pulling, working, working. It is just brutally difficult—mentally and physically. I've done a lot of other sports, and nothing sniffs how hard a canoe race like this is.

So I have to admit I was thankful when I knew we were closing in on the end of the race. Like our previous trip, my parents had agreed to pick us up. With a day left, we calculated the approximate time we would arrive at the Bridgeport Bridge. I called my parents from the same pay phone in Muscoda that we used a year before to arrange our ride home.

The Wisconsin River enters the Mississippi River about 3 miles south of Prairie du Chien. But there isn't a defining spot to mark the river's end. Because no one had really done long-distance timed canoe events, there were no rules to follow. It was simply based on trust. Bill and I chose the Bridgeport Bridge as our finish line because it was the closest landmark that allows river access. The bridge is about 5 miles from the river's end. Because our average speed on the trip was 5 mph, we agreed to add 1 hour to our time to make it as accurate as possible.

ALL-HOURS EFFORT. Wearing a T-shirt custom- designed for the race, Michael Schnitzka grinds out several hours of night paddling.

As we cruised under the Bridgeport Bridge, Bill and I looked at our watches to determine that we paddled the 430-mile Wisconsin River in 6 days, 18 hours. A new world record!

There was no media to greet us. No bands. No cheerleaders. If you really need positive feedback from people at the end of a very long canoe race, don't get into this sport. This type of race is more about training, planning and execution. The race itself is about 5 percent of the entire project. But it really is an amazing feeling when it all

TAKING A BREATHER. Michael Schnitzka pauses near the rushing waters of the Wisconsin River while portaging around a dam in northern Wisconsin.

comes together.

Bill and I shook hands, packed our gear in my parents' car and went home.

———◆———

A few weeks later, I made the drive back to Wenonah Canoe to return the canoe that had made our achievement possible. I showed Mr. Cichanowski a half-dozen articles that had been written about our record-setting race. In almost every one, his company name was mentioned. He smiled.

Later that summer, I read in *Canoe News* magazine that while we were on the water setting our record, two people had set the world record fastest time for paddling the 2,348-mile Mississippi River.

After we were home awhile, I called Bill and double-dog-dared him to go after that record.

He joked with me again, saying, "If you can find a sponsor to pay for everything, I'll do it."

He would—again—learn to regret those words.

JULY/AUGUST, 1984

CANOE NEWS

Volume 17 Number 4

The Eddie Bauer Mississippi River Challenge: Done! 2,348 Miles in Only 23+ Days!

USCA 1984 NATIONAL RACES ★★ AUGUST 18 & 19 ★★

MONUMENTAL MOVE. After the Wisconsin River race described in Chapter 3, this issue of *Canoe News* prompted Michael Schnitzka to up his game and tackle a pro-level challenge.

CHAPTER 4

FIRST YOU CRAWL, THEN YOU WALK, THEN YOU RUN

"If you think adventure is dangerous,
try routine. It is lethal."
~Paulo Coelho

I n the fall of 1987, I called up Bill on the phone. I said, "Bill, do you remember back in 1984 when I said I wanted to paddle the Mississippi River, and you said if I got a sponsor, you would do it? Well, guess what, Bill? I found a sponsor!" He let out a heavy sigh, and I could actually hear the air come out of his lungs.

Through a good connection of my father's, I had set up a meeting with Budget Rent a Car in Milwaukee. The business decided to come on board and sponsor us to go after the Mississippi River world record fastest time in a canoe.

Budget put together a great incentive program for training. We got paid for first-place finishes in local canoe races. To increase the likelihood that we would finish at the top, we picked many short races that the pros don't paddle in. The money we were paid for winning those races allowed us to buy gear we normally could not afford to buy.

I again contacted Wenonah Canoe to ask if they would sponsor us a racing canoe, and the company agreed. This time, though, we didn't have to give back the canoe; this one was given to us gratis. We also sought out many other sponsors to help reduce our costs.

The trip was going to be major-league hard—nothing like the Wisconsin River. The Mississippi River is 2,348 miles long. The longest Bill and I had ever paddled was the 430-mile Wisconsin River. It takes 430 miles to get from the start of the Mississippi River just to Minneapolis.

Anything that happened after the Twin Cities was going to be new to us physically. We immediately started training to get our bodies in shape for something that was going to be incomprehensibly difficult. We knew that only canoeing would not get our bodies ready for such an event. Back then, the term "cross-training" wasn't being used, but Bill and I knew we had to get every part of our bodies ready. So we biked, swam, ran, lifted weights and canoed.

In order to break the record, we would need to limit the number of hours we slept during the race. Instead of setting up camp on shore like we did on our Wisconsin River trip, we decided one of us would paddle the canoe while the other caught some shut-eye in a sleeping bag under the canoe cover. To prepare for napping on the hard bottom of the canoe, a month before the race, I started sleeping on my kitchen floor. Each evening, I threw my sleeping bag on the hard linoleum and crawled inside. It took several days of tossing and turning before I could fall asleep quickly on the uncomfortable surface.

We knew we couldn't attempt this trip alone. There would be no way for us to carry enough food and water to accomplish this goal, so we needed a

THE MISSISSIPPI RIVER is 2,348 miles long and ends 100 miles south of New Orleans.

support crew. Fortunately, we had two friends—Mike Mlynarski and Rod Hanson—who agreed to help. Mike just happened to be looking for a new job, and Rod had some vacation time saved up and asked for a little bit more unpaid leave. To this day, I am amazed I found two friends who were willing to give up a month of their lives to help us accomplish this new world record.

The only navigational aids allowed in a canoe for an adventure race are map and compass. We located highly detailed river maps put out by the U.S. Army Corps of Engineers. I had a friend who worked at Xerox and had the maps copied and reduced in size for Bill and me to carry in the canoe.

Because the Mississippi River has so much boat traffic, we knew the canoe was going to need more lights for safety. Bill started working on wiring up the canoe to have navigational lights on both bow and stern, a headlight, a communication system to the support van, and a music system wired to both seats to keep the boredom away.

Speaking of boat traffic, the Mississippi River has everything from rocky areas to huge shifting sandbars, which make navigation difficult. In the 1930s, Congress authorized the construction of a system of 27 locks and dams via a

RECORD-BOUND. The crew for the 1989 world record race down the Mississippi River included (from left): Rod Hanson, Mike Mlynarski (holding onto door of support van), Michael Schnitzka and Bill Perd-zock. (The dog, Buster, was not present during the race.)

9-foot-deep, 400-foot-wide navigational channel from Minneapolis, Minnesota, to St. Louis, Missouri. With this system, the river depth can be controlled, therefore allowing boats and barges to safely step down or up the river.

Basically, a lock is a huge rectangle-shaped cement box. While locks vary slightly in size, most are 110 feet wide by 600 feet long. On each end, there are two movable doors. The doors on one end swing open to allow a boat to enter the lock, then close after it. To lower the boat, lock operators open a drain valve, allowing water in the lock to spill into the river and lower the water level in the lock. Then the doors on the opposite end of the lock are opened, so the boat can continue down the river. To raise the boat, lock operators open a filling valve, so the water level in the lock rises. Then the doors on the opposite end of the lock are opened, so the boat can continue up the river.

To research the lock and dam system, Bill and I drove to the western part of Wisconsin to investigate how it worked and to watch how boats entered and departed. We noticed that huge whirlpools and boils formed when the massive lock doors opened and closed. We knew to stay clear and allow the water to calm down before we entered and exited a lock.

I contacted Guinness World Records in England and was told we needed to keep a record book and a logbook. The record book should be signed by

STARTING BEFORE SUNRISE. It's 4 a.m. on May 3, 1989, and Bill Perdzock and Michael Schnitzka (front) pose at Lake Itasca, in northern Minnesota, before they take on the Mighty Mississippi. Crew members Mike Mlynarski and Rod Hanson are pictured in back.

people we met along the river to ensure that Guinness could contact these witnesses if needed. The logbook should include notes from our support crew stating the locations, dates and times they saw us during the trip. We hoped all of this preparation and attention to detail would pay off when the time came.

In late April, we drove to Lake Itasca, where the river begins. Our goal was to start May 1, 1989. The area was having a late spring, and many of the lakes were still frozen. We finally started the race May 3.

The Mississippi River had not fully recovered from the historic drought the year before. At its beginning, it is so shallow and so narrow that rocks stick out of the water, allowing you to cross and say you actually walked across the Mississippi River. That is where Bill and I officially started our trip. With our support crew and a few witnesses from the nearby park on hand, Bill touched the rocks and we pushed off. Our very first portage was a mere 30 yards away.

The first 60 miles of the Mississippi flow north to Bemidji, Minnesota. Bill and I had to learn as we went how to handle having a physical support crew on land accompanying us. It took a few days for us to get into a rhythm. At first, we asked to be fed warm food as often as possible, but the logistics made that impossible. We ended up scheduling two resupplies per day, typically around 6 a.m. and 6 p.m. This allowed the support team to go ahead of us, so they could get their rest, prepare our food and take care of any other tasks that had to be done.

We needed to eat constantly, because we burned calories constantly. Bill and I set our watch alarms to go off every 2 hours, 24 hours a day, to remind us to eat. We staggered our mealtimes, so when one of us was eating, the other was paddling. Our diet was very specific. We didn't want the peaks and valleys in our energy levels that come from eating sugar and

SHIPSHAPE SUPPLIES. A custom-made cabinet in the support van holds provisions, including food, beverages, clothing, maps, a microwave and more.

caffeine. We needed sustained energy from proteins and carbohydrates. We also needed foods that were quick and easy to eat, because we could only spare a few minutes for each meal. (See Sample Daily Menu below.)

Our support crew packaged and labeled each of these mini-meals in individual ziplock bags for us, then supplied us with a bagful each morning and evening. Sometimes, the alarm would beep and we'd pull out a bag from our food pack to find that one of the crew had written a smart-ass comment on it: "You'll never make it." "You're slowing down." "You paddle like old people f**k." We'd chuckle when we read these notes, which was often just what we needed during trying times. I remember one instance when Bill was sleeping, and I was paddling by myself in the rain. It was about 3 a.m. and I'm thinking, "Oh, my God, I can't believe I'm out here in this miserable weather." That's when I rifled through the food pack looking for a bag with writing on it—just so I could get a little giggle to lighten my mood.

SAMPLE DAILY MENU

7 a.m. 2 cups fried potatoes or noodles, 2 hard-cooked eggs

9 a.m. Peanut butter and jelly sandwich, sports bar

11 a.m. protein shake, apple

1 p.m. half bagel with cream cheese

3 p.m. half bagel with cream cheese, protein shake

5 p.m. 1 cup sweet potato with 1 teaspoon olive oil, sports bar

7 p.m. 1 cup pasta with sauce

9 p.m. baked potato with butter, protein shake

11 p.m. 1 cup egg noodles, piece of fruit

1 a.m. piece of fruit, ½ cup beans or pasta, protein shake

3 a.m. large muffin, sports bar

5 a.m. 1 cup spaetzle, piece of fruit

When Bill and I first got into canoe racing, we noticed that teams kept hydrated without having to stop paddling. Each racer had a strap around his neck with a small clear tube connected to a water container below his seat. The other end was positioned just below his mouth, so the racer only had to look down slightly to take a sip. It made sense to follow suit on this trip.

We had large water bottles on each side of our canoe seats. When we finished drinking the water in one bottle, we moved the tube to the full bottle. By trickling the water into our bodies slowly, we almost never had to pee. There was almost no waste either, because our bodies were using all the fuel we fed them. We were expending both food and water at the same rate we were taking it in.

Only seeing us twice a day also allowed the support crew time to contact any media that wanted to cover our story as we went through their area. Back then, very few people had cell phones and the World Wide Web wasn't live yet, so Mike and Rod had to make their calls from pay phones.

One of the big concerns Bill and I had was what would happen when we reached a lock and dam. Being a small canoe, how does one enter and exit a lock? What if there are other pleasure craft? Who goes in first? Who exits first?

This is another occasion our support crew came in handy. They drove ahead to locate each lock and dam, and contact the person running it to notify them two canoeists would be coming through in a few hours and needed to pass through the lock quickly. Typically, the lock workers came out to see these two crazy guys trying to paddle the entire river. We always enjoyed meeting new people and trying to explain what we were doing in the short time we were there.

We could typically lock through in about 10 minutes. We were lucky that we only had to portage two locks and dams out of 27. Those two times, we found ourselves behind a line of barges, so we thought it would be quicker to get out and walk than wait. Both times, it took close to 25 minutes.

NO NEED TO PORTAGE. The lock doors in Genoa, Wisconsin, open to allow Michael Schnitzka and Bill Perdzock to paddle into the lock.

The Mississippi River is basically an interstate running north-south in the United States that is full of boat traffic. The lock and dam system ensures that barges can only be so large to fit through the lock. Typically, that would mean one boat (tow) with one engine pushing approximately six to nine boxcars all linked together by chain.

The last lock and dam is a little north of St. Louis. This means for the next 1,200 miles, the river flows freely and picks up speed. It's a whole different ball game. With no locks to worry about, the barges triple and quadruple in size. Imagine having 60 boxcars tied together with three tows pushing them against the current. Each one of the tows after St. Louis had three engines, so that's nine engines pushing. The tows have 7-foot propellers, and with nine of those spinning, you can imagine the waves that are created.

When one of those huge barges would pass, the water displacement was amazing. For a good hour, the water we paddled through was very choppy and wavy. The hardest times were in the middle of the night when it was very dark and sometimes two of these gigantic barges crossed our path at the same time. Bill and I encountered 8- to 10-foot waves coming from all different directions. How we didn't flip over, I still don't know.

———◆———

What amazed our support crew was the lack of roads close to the river after St. Louis. Many people think the Great River Road runs closely along the banks for the entire length of the river, but that is incorrect. Sometimes the road would be 20 or 30 miles away.

There was no GPS in the support van to help Mike and Rod navigate, so they had to buy state maps as they worked their way down the river. For roughly 1,200 miles, most of the land touching the river is privately held by farmers. This meant our support crew was continually asking farmers for permission to get down to the river to resupply us. Twice a day, they regaled us with great stories about the difficulties they had rumbling down dirt roads and through farm fields to find access to the riverbank to reach us. Two different times, the boys got a flat tire that had to be repaired in the closest town they could find. Bill and I loved hearing their reports.

As we headed south, we were getting into much warmer spring air. Since we had started the race with ice on the cover of our canoe, you might think that we'd appreciate the warmth. But on days with the sun beating on us and no wind at all, Bill and I felt like we were in a furnace. We got terribly sunburned. We tried using sunscreen, but it left our hands slippery for hours, making it hard to hang onto the canoe paddles. Eventually, we just stopped wearing it.

With 21 hours of exposure to the elements each day, we had open cuts and blisters on our ears, lips and nose. We didn't dare laugh or smile because our lips would crack open and start bleeding. Despite our rigorous physical training, our arms ached from the constant exertion. Sitting in the canoe day after day took a toll on our backs and legs. A canoe seat looks like a tractor seat. We'd added a layer of foam on top to provide some padding. But it wasn't enough. I can't tell you how much it hurt going through choppy water. It was like shoving a shiv into our butt bones each time the canoe hit a wave.

To dull our aches and pains, we took Tylenol like it was candy, though never more than the 12 tablets maximum recommended. When the race was over, my hands were so cramped from grasping a canoe paddle that it took 2 weeks before I could fully open them. Bill burned out the nerves that run down the sides of his legs from having his feet in foot straps and braced against the sides of the canoe for so long. To this day, the pinky toes on both of his feet are numb.

Like the routine on our previous Wisconsin River trip, we slept only 3 hours a night, but this time in the canoe. I typically slept first. While out on the water, I slowly turned around in the canoe and pulled back the sleep flap. With Bill steadying the canoe, I worked my way back and slipped into our waterproof sleeping bag for some shut-eye. Three hours later, Bill woke me for his sleep shift. We would have to find a spot on shore to switch places. While Bill slept, I moved from my usual spot in the bowman seat to paddle in the backseat, quite a different view for me.

Our goal was to always keep moving, stay awake and stay out of trouble. The times when Bill was sleeping were some of the hardest. It's 2 a.m. and the alarm on my watch goes off. I stop paddling and turn on my headlamp to dig through my food pack. The canoe slowly turns while I gobble down a muffin and an energy bar. When I'm done eating, it's so dark and cloudy that I can't see shore. I'm exhausted and have no idea which way the canoe is pointing. There's no current to indicate which direction the water is flowing. Which way do I paddle? Bill's sleeping and I can't wake him. It's such a frustrating, helpless feeling that for years after this trip, I have recurring nightmares playing out this scenario.

———◆———

We did a lot of research before the race started, but one thing we didn't know was that big oil tankers made their way over 200 miles upriver to reach Baton Rouge, Louisiana. The first time Bill and I saw one of these oil tankers coming upriver, we just about had a heart attack.

We raced quickly to shore to pull the canoe up on land to watch the waves that were created by the gargantuan ship. Being shaped like a canoe, the ship created very symmetrical waves that were not dangerous like those from the huge barges. After a while, Bill and I enjoyed when these ships passed by, because we got to ride the large waves like a roller coaster.

When we reached Baton Rouge—200 miles from the finish—our support crew got on the radio and gave us bad news. They told us we were not going to break the record at our current speed.

That was unacceptable. We had worked so hard, we weren't going to give up now. So we took drastic measures. Bill and I emptied out everything from the canoe, including extra food, extra water, life preservers, a spare battery and even our radio, to lighten the load. We kept nothing in our canoe except drinking water. Without the weight of all that gear, there is less drag when paddling, which would really help. But without a communication system, we couldn't talk to our support crew. We just hoped we'd meet up with them along the way to get food and more water.

Now 200 miles is a long way—about 48 hours of paddling. Generally, with a distance like that, you can't suddenly start digging in and paddling as fast as possible, because you'll never make it to the finish. But Bill and I agreed to paddle until we either ran out of energy or beat the record. We started paddling what we call a "race pace," which means a sprint pace that we'd typically do for a 20-mile, 3-hour race. That's balls-out. When you're done after 3 hours, you're dead tired.

Well, Bill and I did that "race pace" for *48 hours straight*. And it wasn't like a 20-mile race where we started out fresh and had plenty of energy. We were in the 21st day of getting only 3 hours of sleep a night. At this point, we were running on vapors. I can't tell you how difficult it was to maintain that crazy pace. Bill and I were yelling at each other to keep us going. "We gotta try this! We can make this!" We didn't even stop to pee. We just peed in our canoe seats.

ROLLER-COASTER RIDE. Near Baton Rouge, Louisiana, the paddlers handle the waves created by one of many huge oil tankers that are headed out to sea.

This was it.

Heading south out of Minneapolis, the U.S. Army Corps of Engineers has placed mile markers along the banks of the Mississippi River for riverboat captains to use. That made it easy for us to know exactly where we were on our maps at all times.

With the limited amount of brain power we could pull together at this point, Bill and I decided to check our speed to see if our efforts were making a difference. At a mile marker, we set a timer on one of our watches, then we paddled for 15 miles and stopped the watch. We were in a state of sheer exhaustion, so trying to do the math and calculate our speed was like trying to sew together Jell-O. But if our estimates were correct, we were, in fact, narrowing our deficit to break the record.

Have you ever had that feeling as you get close to the end of a destination that the miles seem to get longer? That's exactly how it felt to us.

Everyone thinks the river ends in New Orleans, but the actual stopping point is 100 miles south. The last town heading south on the Mississippi is called Pilottown. That's where our support crew rented a small shrimp boat with the last of our money to follow us to the very end.

The last mile marker we saw before the finish had the number 9 on it. Bill

ONLY 9 MILES TO GO. It's Day 23 when Michael Schnitzka and Bill Perdzock paddle by Mile Marker 9 as they close in on the home stretch of their 2,348-mile Mississippi River race.

and I were averaging about 6 miles an hour paddling. So, a little bit more than an hour after seeing that marker, we finally saw a big wooden piling with nothing on it. When we finally touched Mile Marker 0, we broke the existing world record by *only 29 minutes.*

The support crew helped Bill and I get our canoe into the shrimp boat and off we went for Pilottown. Once there, we loaded up the support crew's van. There were no family members or other people to welcome us. And once again, no bands or cheerleaders to celebrate our achievement. No media to write about our new world record. Nothing.

These things are not fun. At the end, all you can think is, *Thank God this is over.* Bill and I looked at each other and shook hands, but we were barely able to hold the grip because our hands were killing us. The support crew shook hands with us for a job well done, then we all said, "Let's go home."

People have asked me, "How can you paddle 2,348 miles?" And I tell them, "I can't. I can comprehend paddling only 5 miles. I can only do an hour in my brain. That's it."

You've probably heard the old joke: "How do you eat an elephant? Answer: One bite at a time." That's how you have to approach a race like this. At the beginning of the race, if you try to grasp what you're about to do, you will get out of the canoe. You will not start the race, especially if you've done an event like it in the past and know how painful it is.

When you're done, everything hurts. Your whole body is sore, even your legs and feet, which haven't undergone the same brutal workout as your upper body. When I got out of the canoe at the end of this trip, my feet had not touched ground in almost a week. Oh, my God, they hurt. Think of how pruney your skin gets after spending an hour in a hot tub. Then think how your feet would feel after being wet for 23 days. I couldn't believe how sore they were.

FINISH LINE. Michael Schnitzka and Bill Perdzock reach Mile Marker 0, signifying the end of the Mississippi River.

50

At home, I gathered all our information: the logbook, the record book and the many articles that were published that our families received back home. I sent it all to Guinness World Records to review.

Three months later, I came home to find a package leaning against my door. I could clearly see the return address of England and knew it was my Guinness World Records certificate.

Much to my surprise, when I opened the envelope, I found all the information I had submitted. Also inside was a letter stating that our trip was not recognized as a world record due to errors in our support materials. I stood there for the longest time…speechless. I was stunned, upset, furious and confused. Without saying it, the letter suggested we could have cheated.

You see, when Bill and I were paddling through the Memphis area, we encountered 3 days of severe weather. Our support crew could not find anyone

> "These things are not fun.
> At the end, all you can think is,
> 'Thank God this is over.'"

along the riverbanks to act as witnesses and sign the logbook stating they saw us. So basically, Guinness implied we cheated when we broke the record. Bill and I are not cheats. I was not going to let 2 years of training, our sponsors, our support crew, and our support from friends and family go to waste.

In the letter, Guinness suggested we obtain a letter of confirmation from the American Canoe Association. I put together a spreadsheet showing our average speed for the entire race. I could calculate our speed because every time our support crew saw us, they logged it in the book. It was clear from the numbers that during the stretch in Memphis, when paddling during the storms, our speed was cut in half for more than 3 days. I sent a packet to the ACA and included articles and letters from prominent people in my city, including the police chief and the president of a bank. Soon, we received a reply from the ACA acknowledging we did, in fact, set a new time record.

Life was getting busy for me as I started a new career and moved a few times, but I finally reapplied for our world record in February 1992. I sent back the

CERTIFICATE

GUINNESS BOOK OF RECORDS

BILL PERDZOCK & MIKE SCHNITZKA

MISSISSIPPI RIVER CANOE RECORD

2,348 MILES

23 DAYS, 9 HOURS AND 51 MINUTES

3-26 MAY 1989

PETER MATTHEWS   NORRIS McWHIRTER

THIS CERTIFICATE DOES NOT NECESSARILY DENOTE AN ENTRY INTO THE GUINNESS BOOK OF RECORDS

CERTIFIED BY GUINNESS. Only after Michael Schnitzka submits additional materials with his team's average paddling speed does Guinness recognize their Mississippi River race as a world record.

original information along with my letter from the ACA.

A couple of months later, in April, I received a note stating there was a package waiting for me at the post office. As soon as I arrived and saw the large, thin envelope, I knew it was our certificate.

Guinness included a very nice congratulatory letter stating I was right to send the information showing that we actually lost time. The new world record for canoeing the entire Mississippi River was now 23 days, 9 hours and 51 minutes. While Bill and I didn't need a piece of paper confirming our accomplishment, it was still very satisfying to be acknowledged for our hard work.

It wasn't long after returning from our Mississippi River trip that I heard about a bicycle race from San Diego to Annapolis, Maryland. The Race Across America (RAAM) was a 3,000-mile nonstop race that needed great training, top-of-the-line equipment and a support crew. I remember the phone call I made to Bill double-dog-daring him.

I said, "Come on, Bill. Let's do it on a two-man bicycle. Let's hold the time record going down and across this great country. We would be the first ever to do that. Think of the shaving cream commercials we could do."

I was waiting for Bill's timeless reply. This time, I got a, "Hell, no!"

Undeterred, I said, "What if I got a sponsor?"

He replied, "I'm not falling for that again."

In my mind, I replied, *Perhaps.*

CHAPTER 5

62 HOURS WITHOUT SLEEP? NO PROBLEM

"You can sleep when you're dead."
~Source unknown

In the summer of 1993, I read an article in the *Milwaukee Journal* about two men from Illinois who paddled the Wisconsin River to set a new record time of 6 days, 3 hours. I called my longtime canoeing partner, Bill, and told him someone had broken our existing time record by 15 hours. I pulled out my trusty double-dog-dare and asked Bill to go back and paddle the Wisconsin River one more time to set an unbeatable record. Bill gave me his typical response: "If you can find a sponsor to pay for everything, I will do it."

Months later, I happily announced Potawatomi Bingo (now Potawatomi Hotel & Casino) in Milwaukee agreed to sponsor us. I could hear the groan in Bill's voice when I called to share the news, because he knew it meant tons of work ahead of us.

You see, when you plan a long-distance canoe race, paddling only takes up about 5 percent of the work. The other 95 percent is an endless list of requirements to prepare for the event. This includes acquiring additional sponsors to help defray costs, obtaining the canoe, support van and other necessary gear, and readying our bodies for the beating they were about to take.

By far the most important and time consuming are the hours spent in the gym. I have tried many sports, from football, wrestling and track to triathlons. Nothing comes close to how brutal canoeing is on your body. But no matter how hard Bill and I trained, our bodies were wrecks after each long-distance race. Training harder allows you to finish faster, but the pain is always there waiting for you at the end.

When Bill and I train for a race, we typically work out at the gym 2 hours every day in addition to our training sessions on the water. One of the things we did during the winter when the water was frozen was to paddle indoors. Bill took two cheap wood paddles and cut off the blades, leaving just the shaft. At the gym, we rigged up a pulley system with weights attached to the bottom of the shaft. This allows us to paddle for hours.

We also get our bodies in shape by improving our diet. We don't drink alcohol, and we don't eat meat, fast food or soft drinks. Basically, if it's not healthy, we do not consume it. We only drink water. We eat fish and chicken— baked not fried—and lots of fruits and vegetables. Come race day, our bodies are burning about as clean as we can get them. That way, when we eat our race provisions while paddling, we are absorbing the most nutrients and energy as possible.

When I phoned Mike Cichanowski at Wenonah Canoe this time, I told him Bill and I were going after a new record on the Wisconsin River and that we had already acquired a major sponsor who would do a great job promoting the event. Mike knew his company name would get a lot of exposure, and instead of any talk of borrowing a canoe, he gladly gave us a very expensive Kevlar racing canoe. In 1984, the canoe we used was priced at

PADDLING A-WEIGH. Michael Schnitzka works out using a system Bill Perdzock devised that allowed the two men to train for their canoe race indoors during the winter when area lakes and rivers were frozen.

$1,500, but now the cost had risen to $2,500. Bill once again wired up the boat so we had a headlight, navigational lights and music to both seats.

I contacted Mike Mlynarski and Rod Hanson, the same two gentlemen who acted as our support crew down the Mississippi River, and asked if they would like to help us set a new record in the state of Wisconsin. They agreed. Because of the pace we wanted to set on this race, we felt adding a third person would be better for safety. Our crew on the Mississippi River record told us of times they drove when they shouldn't have because of exhaustion. So Bill's brother Pete joined our crew.

With the experience Bill and I gained training for the Mississippi River, we set the wheels in motion for setting a record that no one could better. Sure, our goal was to beat the new record of 6 days, 3 hours, but by how much? After paddling the 2,348 miles of the Mississippi River, we had learned a lot—and so had our support crew.

Bill and I knew we could trim a lot of time from the record by not sleeping on shore. The last time we paddled the Wisconsin River, we had spent approximately 30 hours not paddling. With that in mind, our goal was to beat the new time by that amount, which would bring us in at 4 days, 21 hours.

COLD-WEATHER WORKOUT. To keep their balance sharp, Michael Schnitzka and Bill Perdzock head to downtown Milwaukee to get in some winter paddle time on the Milwaukee River.

This would be the third time Bill and I paddled the entire 430 miles of the Wisconsin River, so we knew what to expect. We knew all the portages as well as all the dangerous places on the river. We planned to make pit stops for food and equipment twice a day like we did on the world record race down the Mississippi.

The arrangement was for our support crew to find us at about 6 a.m. and supply us with 12 hours of food and water, a freshly charged battery for the communication radio and any clothing, such as rain gear, we might need. Typically, they would provide river maps, but Bill and I had the river memorized, so that was not necessary. At the 6 p.m. pit stop, in addition to the normal provisions, our crew would give us warmer clothes for the chilly evenings, a headlight and a sleeping bag.

———◆———

Bill and I both work for ourselves. He is a master electrician, and I sell insurance products to financial institutions. This allows us the luxury of adjusting our schedule so we can chase our dreams. After studying the moon phases, we chose May 10, 1995, as the race's start date.

Instead of beginning early in the morning, we planned to leave from the dam at Lac Vieux Desert at 4 p.m. for safety reasons. There is a dangerous part of the river just past Rhinelander, and we knew if we started in the morning, that would place us in the Whirlpool Rapids in the dark, something we knew we had to avoid at all costs.

Unlike our earlier trips, we had a few witnesses to send us off. Plus, for the first time, our major sponsor was present. John Burke, the president of Potawatomi Bingo, drove up from Milwaukee to wish us well. After we hopped in our Wenonah canoe, he yelled, "Go!" and we pushed off. Our plan was to paddle at least 35 hours without sleeping.

ATHLETIC SUPPORTERS. Support crew members (back row from left) Mike Mlynarski, Pete Perdzock and Rod Hanson assist (front row) Bill Perdzock and Michael Schnitzka as the two attempt to set a new world speed record for paddling the 430-mile Wisconsin River.

The perfect weather to set a time record is no wind or rain. Our first two days were sunny with dead-calm winds. This allowed Bill and I to paddle incredibly hard without having to fight the elements. We maintained a blistering pace, one typically done in a much shorter 21-mile sprint race that we had paddled for training.

To streamline our portages, our support crew went ahead to ensure the areas were clean and there were no obstacles in our way. When we got close to a dam, Mike or Rod would be there to point out the exact spot to take our canoe out of the river. He would then jog a little ahead of us to show us the fastest way around the dam and the best location to put the canoe in below the dam.

There were times we beat the support crew to the next dam and portaged it without any assistance. When that happened, we would hear a crackle on the radio as the support crew asked why it was taking so long for us to reach them. We'd inform them we had already passed the spot, and maybe they should hurry up a little. Bill and I relished hearing their sassy reply, which I won't repeat here.

Potawatomi Bingo did a great job lining up media, and we used the canoe's communication system to do frequent interviews while paddling along the river route. Because the boat is fully covered by material and we have what look like kayak skirts around our waists, it is cumbersome to stop paddling to reach something stored inside the canoe. Bill copied the method we used on the Mississippi River race and installed two switches in the canoe that he could turn on and off with his feet. One switch activated the headlight while the other one activated the communication system to the support van. Bill kept a clip-on microphone attached to his shirt to allow him to talk and paddle. He also wired up our music system to allow the support van to be heard over our radio headsets. Sometimes, we would

MEET AND GREET. On the second day of Michael Schnitzka's and Bill Perdzock's attempt to set the Wisconsin River world record, the tribal council of the Potawatomi Indian Tribe waits on shore in Tomahawk to meet the canoeists sponsored by Potawatomi Bingo.

be listening to music and it would cut out to allow the crew to talk to us.

One surprise for Bill and me was catching sight of the president of Potawatomi Bingo as he followed our progress the first 2 days. We saw him and some of his staff occasionally at bridges, waving and hanging a sign that wished us safe passage. As we paddled into the city of Tomahawk, our radio crackled, and our support crew asked us to hug the left shoreline. As we paddled along, Bill and I could see our support van up ahead with a large group of people standing at the end of a pier. Our crew asked us to stop for a minute to meet some important people.

When we stopped, we were introduced to the entire tribal council of the Potawatomi Indian Tribe. They had heard about the great pace we were setting and wanted to meet the two world record holders representing them. After a few pictures were taken, we pushed off to continue to the next dam, about 20 minutes downstream.

As we got close to the portage, we could see a crowd of about a dozen people —including a reporter and film crew from a Wausau news channel—had

> *"Little did we know then our total time sleeping was going to be just 6 hours for the entire race."*

gathered. I must admit that for the first time ever, I felt like a celebrity…well, at least in the canoeing world. As we made the portage, we were stopped and interviewed by the television news reporter. It was fun, but we were wasting time on land, so we quickly jumped back in the canoe.

My first sleep break came 54 hours into the race. But remember, we started at 4 p.m., not at sunrise like we usually did for our races. So I had been awake 62 hours before that break. Bill's first sleep break came 2 hours later, so he had been up an astonishing 64 hours. When Bill finally slid into the sleeping bag and zipped himself in under the tarp, he was so exhausted that sleep came in seconds. Little did we know then our total time sleeping was going to be just 6 hours for the entire race.

Sleep deprivation is an amazing thing. Many have asked what it feels like to push yourself to total exhaustion. I can only compare it to being highly intoxicated while having a pounding hangover at the same time. Simple tasks like tying your shoes or reading a river map are almost impossible. You see things that aren't there, and your hearing slowly goes away. You become a paddling robot.

At some points during a race, you hit these walls at weird times for no reason. It could be sunny and warm out, and suddenly your body says, *I'm done. I can't go any farther.* But you can't give in to that. You have to somehow fight through that. Trying to open up a ziplock bag to get some food when you're exhausted is like trying to thread a needle when you're so tired you can barely keep your eyes open. It gets to the point where you just want to scream because you can't function. And you hit these walls not once during a trip, but dozens of times. Those moments your body asks, *Why are you doing this?* are brutal. Sometimes, you just need to keep moving. Other times, you need to take a 1-minute break, which is like hitting your body's reset button.

I'm a bowman and sit in the front, which means I don't steer the canoe. There were times I would slowly fall asleep while paddling only to be jerked awake by Bill yelling at me. When I'm paddling, I feel a certain tension on my paddle. When this pressure is increasing, I know Bill is hitting a wall and shutting down. I'd say to Bill, "Take a time-out. Get something to eat." If that didn't work, there was always one sure way to wake each other up—by brushing our teeth. There is something about that simple act, when you are really down and out, that's like taking a refreshing shower. I can't really explain why, maybe it's removing those little sweaters from our teeth. But it brought us back around to reality and kept us both moving during difficult times.

We each had a short 2-hour sleep break before another hazardous part of the trip loomed just around the bend. The Wisconsin Dells can be a very dangerous place to canoe because the river is narrow in areas and bordered by tall rock walls. When the large tourism boats pass by, they create big waves that make it difficult to balance in a canoe. We were very lucky to go through that area early in the morning. The weather had changed from calm and dry to cloudy with a steady rain. We snuck through about 6 a.m. without seeing a single boat.

When we reached the final dam at Prairie du Sac, everything changed regarding the weather. A big thunderstorm had passed by and switched the winds from the west. This part of the river also turns to the west. Because of the storm, we were paddling into a very strong 15- to 20-mph headwind. Even though the current at this point on the Wisconsin River picks up speed, the big headwind canceled it out. We were paddling with all our strength, but it felt as if we were standing still.

At times like this, when you know all the bad things that could possibly happen keep piling up, you just have to embrace the circumstances and not let them overwhelm you.

Here I am paddling hard, laughing and yelling at God or whoever is listening, because the wind is getting stronger, and the waves are getting bigger. I'm in the front, so when our racing canoe cuts through these waves, the water literally hits me in the chest—while Bill's in the back, nice and high and dry. I'm soaked, completely drenched, and the water is running down my neck. It gets to the point where I'm swearing like a drunken sailor, and then *another* big wave hits me. I scream, "Really? Is this all you have? C'mon! Just bring it! Because I can take anything you have." And I refuse to give in and just keep digging in with my paddle as I hear Bill laughing behind me.

One of the bigger things I have gotten out of these adventure races is a fresh perspective. When you've overcome big obstacles, tough challenges or

FINAL SECONDS. On May 14, 1995, Bill Perdzock and Michael Schnitzka paddle under the Bridgeport Bridge to set a new record.

adversities like that, it makes regular-life problems seem so trivial. You got a flat tire today. Really? Call somebody, and they'll come and fix it. Done. How hard was that?

———◆———

The Lower Wisconsin turns into a river that looks similar to its starting point in northern Wisconsin. There are hundreds of sandbars constantly shifting from one side to the other because of the wild current. Normally at night, when we came up to an island or sandbar, a quick flash of the headlight allowed me to see which direction the main current was running. But strong headwinds and clouds blocking the full moon's light hampered our progress.

Countless times we made a poor decision in the pitch-dark by paddling down the wrong channel and ending up on a sandbar. We had to turn around and paddle back around the sandbar to the other side to continue our journey. At one point, it was so difficult to find the channel we were forced to stop and wait until the sun came up. Bill and I found our warm support van sitting at a boat launch waiting for us. We took advantage of the break and caught 2 hours of sleep in the van. Once it was bright enough to see across the river, Bill and I

NEW WORLD RECORD HOLDERS! Friends and family gather at the Bridgeport Bridge to congratulate Michael Schnitzka and Bill Perdzock after they shattered the world record by paddling the 430-mile Wisconsin River in 4 days, 2 hours, 22 minutes.

went back to paddling, and once again we could identify the shallow parts we needed to avoid.

There are hundreds of islands along the way to the Mississippi River, and Bill and I did our best to hide behind them while paddling to get out of the incredibly strong headwind. Although we wanted to stay in the main channel, the waves and wind slowed us down too much. So we aimed for the closest island in front of us, hoping the trees on the island would buffer us from the wind a bit.

As we rounded the last curve to the Bridgeport Bridge, we glimpsed a large crowd of friends and family who had gathered to watch our finish. When we finally paddled under the bridge, we had smashed the existing record by 49 hours and had even surpassed our goal by almost 19 hours! The new time to beat was 4 days, 2 hours and 22 minutes.

After some champagne was popped and pictures were taken, we loaded up the gear on top of the van and headed home.

———◆———

After performing a physically demanding activity, many people experience soreness that lasts a few days. It's your body's way of letting you know that your muscles need a rest. When you are competing in an ultramarathon sport, you don't have the luxury of downtime. You must push yourself until you finish the race or your energy is tapped out. But the consequences of doing that hit hard when you're done.

It was about 6 hours after Bill and I stopped paddling that the support van returned us home. We looked like corpses after rigor mortis had set in. It felt like every muscle in our bodies had frozen up. We couldn't move our fingers and could barely flex our arms. Adrenaline, long gone from our bloodstream, no longer masked the pain of the stress we had inflicted on our bodies. Our aching backs screamed for the comfort of a hot bath, but that would have to wait. The support crew went home, and Bill and I were left to take apart the equipment and store it away for perhaps another time.

This is the letdown that follows any race. The euphoria at setting a new world record was gone, and in its place were physical and mental exhaustion. We had put every ounce of effort we had into achieving our goal, and now we had nothing left. I had made no plans for a future race. I had nothing to train for, nothing to look forward to. I had to just sit and feel the void the race had left in my life.

CHAPTER 6

KEEPING UP WITH NAVY SEALS

"Pain is weakness leaving the body."
~U.S. Marine Corps

Y ou might think by reading my story so far that it takes the written word—whether a historical marker or a newspaper article—to motivate me to embark on an adventure. But I don't think it's as simple as that. I have dozens of ideas and dreams running through my mind at any given time: varying athletic events I want to try, extreme tests of my mental and physical endurance, different ways to set myself apart from others or prove something to myself.

Some of my dreams are well thought out and very specific, while others are random thoughts with little substance behind them. But having all these dreams opens me up to opportunities I might not pursue otherwise. That's why I think it's important that each individual have a dream—even one that seems out of reach at the moment. Because you never know when an opportunity will present itself or how following one dream can lead to fulfillment of another.

Did I know that asking to join an adventure team would give me a chance to train with Navy SEALs—men who have undergone the toughest military training in the world? No, I didn't. But that's exactly where my dreams led me.

———◆———

A few weeks after Bill and I set the Wisconsin River world record in 1995, I read in the *Milwaukee Journal* about Juli Lynch, a local woman who was a member of an adventure team. She was a marathon runner by trade but was looking to compete in the Raid Gauloises, a long-distance endurance race in South Africa slated for 1997.

For a few years, I had been dabbling in triathlons in addition to my canoe races. And I was always looking for something new to try. Friends in the canoe world asked if I was interested in one of these long-distance adventure races. After doing a bit of research on them, I wanted to hear more about participating in a multi-sport adventure race like the Raid.

From the newspaper article, I learned the teams were required to have a minimum of five participants with at least one woman on the team, and Juli's team was short a few people. She needed one more member and possibly a backup person in case someone got injured during training.

Intrigued by the challenge of a 500-mile adventure, I contacted Juli and asked if she'd meet me for coffee. She agreed. At our meeting, I shared my resume to see if she would consider adding me to the team. That's also when

> "*These guys are the toughest of the tough. Knowing this, I have to admit I was a bit intimidated by the thought of training with them.*"

I learned the three other members of the team were Navy SEALs. A few days later, Juli called to say the team would take my request into consideration, but I would have to do some training with them first.

To be in the race, teams must be qualified in many areas of adventure racing. Race judges test contestants on all the skills required in the race, and those who do not pass are not allowed to compete for safety reasons. For the Raid, team members needed to know how to rappel down a wall, belay a fellow mountain climber, properly saddle and ride a horse, paddle a canoe, and navigate a raft through rough waters.

Since my experience was on the water, I could help the team be more efficient in canoeing and white-water rafting. But I needed practice in a few other areas. Juli worked at a horse farm in western Waukesha County, so I spent many days there training in the equestrian world.

When I was in the Army, I had learned to rappel and mountain climb, but not to the level that this race was going to need. So I offered to set up a training session for our team. My family has a cabin near Wisconsin Rapids, which is less than an hour south of Wausau and Rib Mountain, the second highest peak in Wisconsin at 1,942 feet. That made it an ideal place for our team to meet one another and practice the skills needed for the race.

In early April of 1996, I called the Milwaukee office of the Boy Scouts of America for contact information for a troop in Wausau. After a few more phone calls, I set up a meeting with the leader of a Boy Scout troop in that area. I explained our team was training for an adventure race, and I asked if his Scouts would put together a mountaineering course at Rib Mountain State Park for us. The scoutmaster loved the idea and said his troop would enjoy planning an outdoor event and the chance to meet the Navy SEALs. I learned there was a quarry on the west side of Rib Mountain and obtained permission from the owner for our team to rappel into his quarry a few times too.

———◆———

The three SEALs flew in from Norfolk, Virginia, to join Juli and me on our drive up to Wisconsin Rapids. Now, I don't know if you're familiar with Navy SEALs and what they do. SEALs are from the Navy's Sea, Air and Land Forces. According to the Navy recruiting website, these men "are expertly trained to deliver highly specialized, intensely challenging warfare capabilities that are beyond the means of standard military forces." We're talking counterterrorism, reconnaissance and combat missions that may be carried out by parachute, submarine, helicopter, boat or on foot. These guys are the toughest of the tough.

Knowing this, I have to admit I was a bit intimidated by the thought of training with them. But it helped that our first day was spent on the water, where I'm most comfortable. I brought along three different racing canoes, and we practiced about 4 hours working on proper paddling techniques and ways to move the canoe through the water more efficiently. Anyone can ride a bicycle, but bicycle racers know how to pedal fast while consuming the least amount of effort. My job that day was to ensure our team moved our canoes through the water smoothly without wasting energy.

On the second day, we donned our backpacks for a long run in the sandy dunes south of Wisconsin Rapids near the town of Rome. Now, I'm not the best runner, but I knew I could train to be ready for the race in a year. Keep in mind, Juli was a marathon runner and the SEALs were active-duty soldiers, so they were in peak physical shape. I kept up with them for about 5 miles, then they slowly pulled away from me. Eventually, they got so far ahead the group looked like a small dot a mile away. Since I didn't want to get separated and lost, I doubled back to the cabin. Hours later, they returned, saying they had logged in *only* 20 miles.

Early on the third day, we drove to downtown Wausau and put our canoes in the Wisconsin River. Juli was not feeling well, so she stayed back at the cabin. The day was going to be all about the guys. The four of us paddled south to Lake Wausau, then against the current up the Rib River until we reached Rib Mountain State Park. There, we were greeted by the entire Boy Scout troop and their leaders. Once we switched from our canoeing gear to our mountaineering gear, we joined the Scouts and their leaders and hiked up the path to the top of Rib Mountain.

I wish I had photos to share of our group of at least 20—the Scout troop in uniforms hiking alongside our team in mountaineering gear. But because the SEALs were active military, neither I nor the Boy Scouts were allowed to take pictures that showed their faces.

At the mountaintop, we were met by a representative of the rock quarry informing us their insurance company would not allow us to rappel into the quarry, so we moved on to the mountaineering portion of the weekend.

In adventure racing, a GPS unit is not allowed, so you must navigate strictly by map and compass. The SEALs explained that when it comes to mountaineering, each man has a specific job while traversing the area. One member counted his footsteps so that at any given time he could tell you how far we had gone. Another member's duty was to handle the compass to ensure we headed the exact direction needed. I had an altimeter watch, so my job was to announce our altitude when asked. Another person carried the topographical map and determined the best route to the next point

The scoutmaster told us the first waypoint was about 800 yards away and gave us the compass heading. We were to look for a tree with a pink ribbon around it. There, we would find a plastic bag with the direction and distance to the next waypoint. He told us there were 14 plastic bags waiting to be found.

With that knowledge, one of the SEALs yelled, "Let's go!" and we started running straight down the mountain through the woods.

Even though it was early May, there was still snow on the north side of Rib Mountain. After a few hours, our team got into a nice cadence, which allowed us to have conversations while working our way from point to point. Don Mann, the lead SEAL, did most of the talking and shared fascinating stories about some of his missions, although he was unable to give details because the information was still classified.

Don is an interesting character. Earlier, while we were changing into our mountaineering gear, he pulled out a large box from one of our sponsors with brand-new leather hiking boots in it. Now most people wouldn't wear new boots for the first time when embarking on a long trek. But Don decided to break in his boots that weekend.

After running for 8 hours straight, crisscrossing Rib Mountain many times and trudging through thigh-deep, almost-frozen muck in swamps more than once, we took a break by our car to resupply. We all took off our boots and socks to put on fresh clothes. I noticed Don struggling to remove his boots. I walked over to see if he was OK and noticed as he pulled off his sock that his

> *"Not only was it a blister, but the skin on top of the blister had come off to expose red, raw flesh."*

entire heel was a blister. Not only was it a blister, but the skin on top of the blister had come off to expose red, raw flesh. I assume the skin was somewhere in his sock.

I watched him search his backpack and pull out some moleskin. If you've done a lot of running or hiking, you know moleskin is a heavy cotton fabric that has a soft, flannel-like surface on the front and adhesive on the back. You attach it to the inside of your shoe to help prevent blisters.

When I saw Don open the moleskin package, I thought it was a little late for that. Then I watched him peel the backing off the sticky side of the moleskin and slap the adhesive directly onto the exposed flesh of his heel. The pain must have been immense, because Don curled into a fetal position and fell over on his side as he tried to bear it. After a minute or so, he sat up, slid on a clean, dry sock and shoved his foot back into the same boot that had caused all the pain.

The rest of the team gathered to watch Don remove the other boot. His Navy SEAL buddies good-naturedly ribbed him, knowing the pain he would soon endure with his other foot, and they relished in it. Perhaps the special forces enjoy that type of pain, or maybe seeing their leader in a weak moment made them happy. Either way, they giggled so much I had to join in. Don didn't find the humor in it, knowing he had to repeat the process, slapping the sticky moleskin on his other exposed heel, pulling on a clean sock and shoving his foot back into the boot. The pain on his face was indescribable as he cinched up his boot strings.

After we refilled our water containers and ate some granola bars, we were ready to seek out the next waypoint. I watched Don get off the ground and take

ELUSIVE PATCHES. Boy Scouts leave these Rib Mountain Trail patches in the last plastic bag—the only bag that Michael Schnitzka and the Navy SEALs didn't find.

a few steps. He looked like a 90-year-old man getting out of a chair. Don had led the pack the entire day, but when we started out again, he brought up the rear. Amazingly, after about an hour, he worked his way up again to be the lead man out in front.

THE WEIGHT OF THE WORLD. Michael Schnitzka carries his canoe while competing in a canoe biathlon a month before he broke his collarbone while training on his bike.

We trained through the night. The only things lighting our way were our battery-powered headlamps. We must have looked funny to vehicles out in the country as we occasionally crossed the road: four guys with backpacks in a line, jogging short distances only to dart into the woods now and again. Don kept things interesting for me by recounting recent missions, although he left out exact locations and other classified details. So many times during that weekend, I thought to myself how exciting it was to be in the presence of the most highly trained warriors on the planet.

It was about 3 p.m. the following day when we began searching for our last plastic bag. We weren't lost, but we could not locate our target. We fanned out into a small skirmish line, crisscrossing a small group of trees where that last bag had to be. Because we were so tired, we decided to halt our search and make a beeline to the area where the Scout troop had parked our cars.

When we finally stopped, we had been running up and down and across Rib Mountain for 34 hours straight with only one rest stop. Don said he was impressed with my endurance and how I kept up with our country's top-of-the-line soldiers. I felt slightly redeemed after tapping out the previous day on their 20-mile warmup run.

But I was the one who was really impressed with what these incredibly physically fit men could do, not just on a course created by Boy Scouts, but in the field, under pressure and often in enemy territory with the chance of being injured or killed at any moment. And I still had the impression that the SEALs really didn't work that hard during our Rib Mountain training session. On the other hand, I did everything I could just to keep up with them. I'm certainly glad these warriors are on our side when the world needs highly trained individuals in tip-top shape. These guys are flown in, usually at night, to perform dangerous work without a thank-you needed nor requested.

A few days after I got back and the SEALs had returned to their base, I called the scoutmaster to thank him for organizing our mountaineering exercise. He asked me what we thought of the gifts the Scouts had left for us.

I asked, "What gifts?"

He said, "The really nice colorful jacket patches that were in the last plastic bag."

I confessed that the last bag was the only one we couldn't find.

About a week later, the patches arrived in the mail. I kept one, threw the others in an envelope and mailed them off to my teammates on the East Coast. They wrote back thanking me for a great training session.

◆

In late July, while I was training on my bicycle, I hit a rock in the road, flipped my bike and broke my left collarbone. I remember the call I made to our team captain, Don Mann, explaining my broken bone. He just laughed and told me to rub some dirt on it.

The thought of throwing on a heavy backpack and tightening down the shoulder straps made my head spin. I knew, however, the pain would be gone by race day, and the injury wouldn't slow me down as I continued to train my legs. The race was still 6 months away, so I was confident I would be back to 100 percent by then.

About 2 months after my accident, our team got bad news that our major sponsor, who had agreed to contribute $70,000, had pulled out, and we would be unable to compete in the Raid. While our team was very disappointed, there was nothing any of us could do. Finding a new major sponsor before the race was impossible. But I later heard through the grapevine that Don and Juli finally did get to compete together in a different endurance race—the Eco-Challenge in Queensland, Australia, in 1997.

———◆———

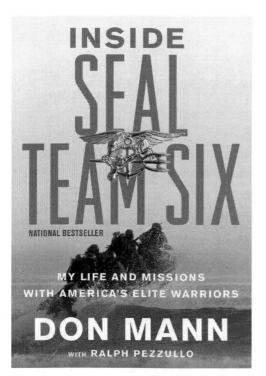

YEARS AFTER TRAINING with Don Mann, Michael finds out Mann was a member of SEAL Team Six. (*Book cover used with permission of Don Mann.*)

Fast-forward 7 years. It's 2013, and I'm watching a television show on the Navy SEAL team that took down Al-Qaeda leader Osama bin Laden in Pakistan on May 2, 2011. For the first time, the U.S. government confirmed SEAL Team Six—the best of the best Navy SEALs—was responsible.

The television program featured interviews with former SEAL Team Six members. Much to my surprise, Don Mann—the person I trained with up and down Rib Mountain—was among those interviewed.

In fact, all three SEALs I trained with were members of SEAL Team Six, so I'm very proud I had the opportunity to train with them.

I contacted Don Mann through Facebook to express my delight that I'd had the privilege to train with the best of the best. He replied and sent me an autographed copy of his 2012 autobiography: *Inside SEAL Team Six: My Life and Missions with America's Elite Warriors.*

To my surprise, many of the stories he told while we were running up and down Rib Mountain were included in his book. If you get the chance to read the book, you will notice something right away that's quite different. Many sections of his book are heavily redacted. The intelligence community previewed the book before it was published and blacked out all the classified or sensitive information. When I read it, I smiled a bit knowing that I had listened to Don's stories close enough that I could fill in some of the blanks.

He signed the book for me and wrote a short message:

Mike,
You have been such a great inspiration to me. I greatly respect all you have done in the world of ultrasports.
Your friend,
Don Mann

While I didn't make it to the race in South Africa, I got the chance to train with the top soldiers on the planet. Some people might look at this as a failed dream. I look at it as I chased after something.

You've probably heard the old saying, "When you fall off a horse, you have to get back in the saddle." I hate repeating it, but it really is so true in life. Don't allow a failure to stop or even slow you down. Look at failure as a learning opportunity.

You will always find forks in the road of life. Sometimes, when one path ends, another begins.

You must squeeze as much as you can into every moment, because **tomorrow is promised to no one.**

CHAPTER 7

THE AGONY
OF DEFEAT

*"Without disappointment,
you cannot appreciate victory."
~Memphis Raines, Gone in Sixty Seconds*

I was disappointed that our adventure team never got the chance to compete in the Raid Gauloises. But I never felt defeated by the circumstances. In fact, I'd rarely tasted defeat. As a team, Bill and I had been successful in all the dreams we had chased. I felt we accomplished that by careful planning, using the best equipment possible and having a top-notch support crew with tons of experience. Unfortunately, our next adventure would introduce us to a new and unwelcome feeling: failure.

If you look at some older editions of Guinness World Records, the only record under canoeing that's noticeable was set by the British Royal Air Force canoe team. The team set the record time for paddling the Rhine River in 10 days, 3 hours.

The record that Bill and I set on the Mississippi River was mentioned only once in the 1993 edition of the book. I think it's because the Guinness World Records book is published in England, so naturally it makes sense to show off citizens from the publisher's native country.

No matter what people tell you, when they accomplish something difficult or noteworthy, they want to be rewarded in some way. It need not be a monetary reward; a simple recognition of the achievement is often enough. While Bill and I don't break records just to get into the book, if we do beat a record that is published somewhere, we would like the record updated to reflect that we bettered that time. That got me thinking: if we were really going to get our name into Guinness, maybe we should think European and go after the Rhine River world record.

The Rhine River starts in the small tourist town of Chur, Switzerland, which is one of the oldest cities in Europe with its history dating back over 5,000 years. The Rhine River then flows north for about 720 miles, touching six countries: Switzerland, Austria, Liechtenstein, Germany, France and Holland.

That means the Rhine is more than twice the length of the Wisconsin River and only a third the distance of the Mississippi River. Bill and I had set world records on both U.S. rivers. Why not try for international fame? Using the experience Bill and I gained from the two races down the Wisconsin River and our world record Mississippi River race, we felt we could trim 3 days off the existing time of 10 days and 3 hours.

I again dared Bill to go after that Rhine River record, and he said, "If you get a sponsor to pay for everything, I'll think about it."

———◆———

A friend of mine had a connection to Hofbräu München brewery in Munich, Germany. After a bit of correspondence with him and the beer manufacturer, we set up a meeting in Munich. I immediately placed a call to Mike Cichanowski at Wenonah Canoe and told him we planned to attempt the world record on the Rhine River. He was very excited about the possibility

THE RHINE RIVER starts in the town of Chur, Switzerland, and flows 720 miles north to the North Sea.

of his product being paddled at 6 mph by millions of people living along the banks of the Rhine. Without hesitation, he once again agreed to supply us with another expensive, lightweight Kevlar racing canoe.

Bill, my friend and I flew to Munich to have a meeting with representatives of Hofbräu München. They agreed to transport our canoe from the U.S. to Switzerland and back in a shipment of half barrels of beer. They also would provide a van for our support crew. After our meeting, we traveled to Chur to locate the beginning of the Rhine River. We worked our way downriver, looking at all the potential dangerous spots we would encounter.

The Rhine River has 11 locks and dams very similar to those on the Mississippi. Bill and I could not ensure that we would be able to lock through like a ship, so we had to find all the portage entries and exits. The last lock and dam is 287 miles into the race. That leaves 433 miles of free-flowing water. A potential concern was that the Rhine River is much narrower than the Mississippi River but has almost twice the river traffic.

After we returned home, Bill and I designed a wooden box to carry our 18-foot, 6-inch canoe and all of our gear. It looked like three huge coffins glued together. Hofbräu München contacted me shortly after and shared the stacks of paperwork that would need to be completed and the regulations that had to be followed to ship our container, one of which was a bromide fumigation certificate. We had to spend $500 to place our big wooden box in a room to have a bug bomb set off to ensure there were no living insects in it.

When I was once asked the difference between being in Europe and in the United States, I explained that in the U.S., you can do whatever you want unless a sign says you can't. In Europe, especially Germany, you can't do anything you want unless a sign says you can. So the details to pull off this race were endless and confusing.

Another complication was the time difference, with Germany being 8 hours ahead of us. It would sometimes take days to get a reply to a question. When our shipping day finally arrived, Bill and I transported the canoe box on a trailer to a huge beer distributor in Chicago. We were relieved two weeks later when we received confirmation from Hofbräu München that our canoe had arrived and was safely in storage at the brewery just outside Munich.

Just like our previous races, we did as much research as we could on the Rhine's water levels. We wanted to race when there would be enough—but not too much—water for the river to be dangerous. I even located a European canoe and kayak store that offered trips down local rivers including the Rhine. They agreed that early April would be the perfect time to attempt such a race. Then we double-checked that there would be a full moon to provide some light at night.

———◆———

On March 30, 2007, Bill and I, along with our longtime two-man support crew of Mike Mlynarski and Rod Hanson, flew to Munich. A representative from Hofbräu München met us at the airport to drive us to the brewery to pick up the sponsored support van. Because the van could only hold three people, one of us would have to take a train instead from the airport to Switzerland. I drew the short straw so Bill, Mike and Rod left in the van with plans to meet me in Chur. Our third support crew member, Sebastian Schmidt, planned to fly in a few days later to join us.

Neither my crew nor our canoe had arrived by the time I hopped off the train in Chur. I walked from the station to the designation point and waited about an hour until a flatbed truck showed up to deliver our canoe box. The driver didn't want to wait for my crew to arrive, so he used the small crane on his truck to lift the huge canoe box from the truck and place it right on the sidewalk in downtown Chur. We opened the 20-foot box and emptied it, then he returned it to the back of his truck before departing.

There I sat alone on the sidewalk, alongside our canoe and hundreds of pounds of gear. I waited…and waited…and waited. It was not an auspicious start to our adventure.

When Bill, Mike and Rod finally arrived around midnight, they were 4 hours late. A large accident had occurred in one of the tunnels leading to Chur. There was no way for the van to turn around, so the crew had to wait for emergency equipment to arrive and clean up the mess. In those early morning hours, we packed our gear in the van, tied the canoe to the roof and set off for the hotel where the city's tourism bureau had graciously provided rooms for us to stay in.

The next day was very busy as we had to prepare our gear, charge our batteries and do a lot of food shopping. We even met the mayor of Chur, who presented us with a message in a bottle that he wanted us to deliver to the mayor of Rotterdam, Holland. That night, the tourism bureau also bought us dinner. Bill's parents happened to be in Switzerland at the time visiting friends, and they were able to join us for the festivities. It was the first time Bill and I ever had family members present to watch us start one of our adventures.

The following morning, we started our race. But the water levels Bill and I had predicted weren't there. The area around Chur, known for great snow skiing, had very little snow or rain from January through April, causing the river water levels to be lower than usual. Because the Rhine River drops over 500 feet in elevation in the first 50 miles, it has a really fast current no matter what the water levels. But low water levels expose more rocks, which cause even more dangerous white-water rapids.

Bill and I were using a flat-water racing canoe, not a white-water canoe. Because we were only able to ship one canoe, we had to choose the one that we were going to use most of the time. We knew the first 50 miles would be difficult, due to the elevation drop, fast current and numerous rapids.

But the water was even more dangerous than we had expected. Bill and I had paddled a few miles and were navigating an area of swift rapids when we saw a small but fast stream joining the Rhine. As we paddled by, the crosscurrent produced by the stream entering the river hit us broadside and flipped our

READY FOR THE RHINE. In Switzerland before the race, the crew re-creates a photo from the 1989 Mississippi River race. From left are Rod Hanson, Mike Mlynarski (holding onto door of Hofbräu München-sponsored support van), Michael Schnitzka and Bill Perdzock.

canoe. One second, we're paddling hard, and the next, we're submerged in frigid water. What a shock to our bodies! I don't know the exact temperature of the water, but keep in mind it's all runoff from the snow in the mountains surrounding the area. Cold tap water from a kitchen faucet is typically 50°, and this water was so much colder.

I tried to gain my footing on the river bottom to help guide us to shore, but the current was so fast I never had a chance. What made it worse was that Bill and I couldn't just turn over the canoe and hop back in it. We had to hang onto the overturned canoe as it moved through the rapids until we reached a smooth section of the river. Then we pulled it to shore and dumped out the water. It was fortunate that neither of us were injured.

Bill and I stripped off our clothes and used our bare hands to wring out as much of the bitterly cold water from our clothing as we could. We knew that even though our clothes were still wet, putting them back on and paddling again would help raise our body temperature quickly. Bill and I had been through worse situations, so we pushed off from shore and plowed on.

About 5 miles later, the unthinkable happened: we flipped again. This time, we were carried downstream a long way—about a half mile, or to put it into

LOW BLOW. After pushing off in Chur, Switzerland, Bill Perdzock and Michael Schnitzka are troubled to find the Rhine River has unexpectedly low water levels due to a lack of snow.

perspective, two times around the track at a football field. We made it to a sandbar and pulled the boat out of the water. We were soaked to the skin, and I could feel a bone-chilling cold seeping into my limbs. While removing our clothes again to squeeze out the water, I saw a look in Bill's eyes that I have never seen before.

Bill is easily the toughest man I know. He is almost impervious to pain, and if he is hurt, you would never know it because he'd never tell you. But at that moment, he stared at me with a look I can only describe as fear. I'm quite sure

> *"At that moment, Bill stared at me with a look I can only describe as fear. I'm quite sure I was giving him the same look."*

I was giving him the same look. But I wasn't ready to give up. Instead, I put on my best poker face and started laughing. I said, "Bill, I'm getting a little tired of swimming. Do you think you could do a better job at paddling?" He cracked a smile, and within a few minutes, we were back at it again.

Despite paddling hard for several miles, our bodies had not warmed up from our underwater plunges. We were only about 20 miles into the 720-mile race when our canoe overturned a third time. The blast of icy water hit us full-force, making it difficult for our numb fingers to even grasp onto the canoe.

Our support crew happened to be on shore nearby, and they could see us struggling. They rushed down to the water to grab us and pull our canoe onto the rocks. They noticed Bill and I were shivering badly and our lips were turning blue.

We were very far behind schedule, and the water ahead was expected to be even more dangerous. So our support crew canceled the race due to safety concerns. Bill agreed with them, but I just couldn't believe the race was over that fast. I tried to come up with ideas that would allow us to keep going. I even suggested putting heavy rocks in the canoe to weigh it down and make it harder to flip. But had we done that and then flipped again, the canoe probably would have sunk to the bottom.

So there it was: the first failure for Bill and me. It was both humbling and humiliating since we had never failed at setting a record before.

We packed up our gear and drove to the end of the first section of the Rhine

River near the city of Bregenz in Austria. There, the river enters a very large body of water called Lake Constance or *Bodensee* in German. It was high on our list of areas that could give us trouble because of its shallow waters and unpredictable winds.

We parked near where the river enters to find the lake was glass-calm with not a hint of wind in the air. I remember sitting by the lake, questioning where our planning went wrong and what we could have done differently. But I knew the answer and I didn't like it. No matter how hard you plan, physically train or do your research, there is always the unpredictable part of these adventures. You have to realize sometimes things happen that are out of your control and the only thing you can do is accept it.

We took our gear straight back to Munich to the Hofbräu München brewery, dropped off the support van and packed up our box. We rented a vehicle and spent the next few days sightseeing in southern Germany. One of my fond memories was taking the team to the Hofbräuhaus. Our goal was to set the world record on the Rhine River, then celebrate at the beer hall with free drinks and some media coverage. Now, we sat there like any other tourists, drinking wonderful beer and listening to a polka band.

On the plane ride home, I kept reviewing our notes and maps. I figured if

FIRST FAILURE. Bill Perdzock scans the calm waters of Lake Constance as Michael Schnitzka (head bowed) and crew member Mike Mlynarski contemplate the race they were unable to finish.

we came back with a much more stable canoe, we could handle any water conditions. Our overall time would be slower, but it's impossible to set a new record if you don't even finish the race. I know it really bothered Bill that we had failed. He is a quiet man and does not show his emotions as easily as I do, but I know it really affected me.

While Bill takes care of the mechanical end of these adventures, I take care of the business end. I had acquired many sponsors who provided a lot of equipment for us to use. I had lined up media attention for most of the race. I had television, radio and newspaper people waiting for us to paddle through their areas. We had the mayor of Rotterdam waiting for his message in a bottle, and I'm quite sure he had some media ready to document that. We had our friends and family back home waiting to see us set a new time record.

Maybe I'm putting too much pressure on myself, but when we failed, I felt as if I let down all of those people. That feeling of failure has never gone away; I've just done the best I can to not let it eat me alive. I had to try to let it go and move on.

The saddest part for me was returning home from Europe, sitting on my couch and knowing that at that exact moment, we would still be paddling on the Rhine River had things not gone wrong. That is a feeling I never want to have again.

I initially avoided discussing the trip. Friends convinced me it would be OK to talk about our failed attempt. When I did, people were very supportive. Most said they could never imagine trying such a difficult endeavor. To them, that we gave it our best shot was victory enough. I, however, felt much differently. But I'm learning to overcome that feeling of failure and be grateful for the opportunity to even try to break the record.

"I can accept failure. Everyone fails at something. But I can't accept not trying."
~Michael Jordan

CHAPTER 8

A TEACHABLE MOMENT

*"Life moves pretty fast. If you don't stop
and look around once in a while, you could miss it."*
~Ferris Bueller, Ferris Bueller's Day Off

I was crushed by our unsuccessful Rhine River attempt—our first defeat—and that failure still haunts me to this day. But it doesn't define me. I am not one to wallow in my disappointment. I don't see the point in it. It doesn't change the past. For me, the best way to move on from defeat is to learn from it.

That's why when I asked Bill if he would try the race again, I didn't take his first "no" for an answer. I gave him a few more weeks, then called to ask him again if he would like to make a second attempt at the record. I went to visit him at his house, and over his kitchen table, I threw out my trusty, never-failed-yet, double-dog-dare. He informed me his wife was pregnant and he couldn't run around the globe chasing dreams because he had to concentrate on his family. Although I was disappointed, I understood. Losing Bill as my partner was a huge setback, but I wouldn't let it stop me from pursuing my dream. I had to move on to find a new partner. But who would be crazy enough to join me?

Later that fall, I was fishing with an old buddy of mine and asked him if he knew anyone who might be interested in canoeing with me. He suggested a friend of his daughter's and told me the young man, Dan Hoffmann, was a rock climber and kayaker. Dan was fresh out of college with an outdoor education degree and was working at a children's camp in Minocqua in northern Wisconsin.

When I finally got a chance to meet Dan, I explained the records I had set and my desire to try the Rhine River world record again. Dan had a lot of kayaking experience, but he wasn't familiar with the world of flat-water marathon canoe racing. Even after I told him how difficult the training and the race would be, he was still interested.

To even consider another try, I needed to find a sponsor to help defray the costs of shipping our equipment and a canoe to Germany. Once again, I reached out to Mike Cichanowski, the president of Wenonah Canoe. I didn't know at that time that Wenonah sold canoes in Germany, so when I asked Mike if he knew anyone who might be interested in helping us achieve our goal, he asked me if he could be our main sponsor. I was delighted with the offer and immediately said "yes." This put the wheels in motion for us to pursue the Rhine River world record time.

———◆———

Anyone can pull on a canoe paddle, but can you train a person to pull on a canoe paddle 21 hours a day for 7 days? I certainly hoped so. To achieve a world record, Dan also needed to understand water hydraulics, to learn to read the river water and to know how to get the most speed out of the river as possible. He also had to become skilled at reading a river map in the dark and pinpointing our location at all times, just by using a map and compass. It would be a steep learning curve, so we planned to train in the spring and summer of 2010.

I signed us up for a few canoe races of about 20 miles in length to give Dan opportunities to learn how to make the canoe go as fast as possible for short periods of time. We also took two long adventures on the Wisconsin River to give him the experience of paddling through the night while only taking very short breaks.

During the training runs, I had Dan pick the exact routes to take on the map without any help from me. There would be times on the Rhine that I'd be under the tarp sleeping and Dan would be 100 percent on his own. He needed to know how to handle situations by himself while being very tired and hungry.

On one of our training runs on the Wisconsin River, Dan chose to go around an island on a route I knew would lead to a dead end. Remember, Bill and I had paddled the Wisconsin River three times, and we got to know it quite well. In this particular area, there are many islands, the main channel is hard to find and it's very difficult to determine your location on the map. So it's easy to understand how Dan picked the wrong route.

Because I'm in the front of the canoe, Dan could not see me smiling as we paddled a good 6 miles the wrong way. Sure enough, about an hour later when we reached the dead end, Dan realized his error and we had to turn around to paddle the 6 miles back just to get on course.

It was clear Dan was angry and discouraged by his mistake. When you're physically working hard and getting more fatigued by the minute, the thought of retracing your steps is very frustrating. You can't describe this feeling to somebody; you need to experience it. I believe it was important that Dan felt that anger and disappointment. Only after our training run was complete did I tell him I knew we were going the wrong way the whole time. He didn't say anything, but he didn't seem to find quite the same amount of humor in it as I did.

———◆———

THE DISTANCE across Lake Michigan from Manitowoc, Wisconsin, to Ludington, Michigan, is 51 miles.

One of the things I've always wanted to try was to set the fastest paddling time across Lake Michigan in a canoe. For years, Bill and I tried to find the right time to do that, but it just never came to fruition. I suggested to Dan that we try to set a small record before going after the Rhine River, and he agreed.

Lake Michigan has a maximum length of 307 miles and a maximum width of 118 miles. Its narrowest width—from Rawley Point Lighthouse in Two Rivers, Wisconsin (a stone's throw from Manitowoc) to Big Sable Point Lighthouse in Ludington,

Michigan—is 51 miles. Our goal was to meet or beat the current 26-hour canoeing record between those two points.

In order to do that, the lake conditions had to be in our favor. In August 2010, conditions lined up that it was going to be perfectly flat on the water in a few nights. John Udvare, a neighbor of mine who owned a boat, offered to act as our support crew. With a 2-day notice, I contacted Dan in Minocqua and told him we had a chance to go after the Lake Michigan record. John and I drove to Two Rivers, pulling his boat with my canoe on top of the car while Dan drove from Minocqua to meet us.

All the research I had done on lake and weather websites said the night of August 15 was going to be dead calm on Lake Michigan. About 9 p.m., Dan and I pushed off from the beach at the lighthouse in Two Rivers in our 19-foot Wenonah Itasca canoe and started paddling east. John was in the support boat nearby, keeping an eye on us in the dark. We were lucky to have a full moon that night, which happened strictly by chance.

An hour into paddling, we started feeling occasional light gusts of wind in our faces. Over the next couple of hours, the small gusts increased to a steady wind, which turned into a strong headwind from the east. Dan and I encountered 15-mph winds, which turned the rough 2-foot waves into brutal 3-foot waves. After 4 hours of strenuous paddling, about 20 miles into our 51-mile adventure, we came to the disappointing realization that our record attempt was over. The wind and waves had slowed our speed to such a degree we knew we could no longer beat the record. We got into the support boat, slid the canoe on it and motored back to Two Rivers.

Our first attempt at the Lake Michigan record failed. I asked Dan afterwards how he felt about not making it across the lake. He said he was fine with it, because sometimes nature doesn't always follow the rules. This young buck was already wise beyond his young years.

———◆———

Just 2 months later, in early October, I was checking the weather forecasts and noticed that another high-pressure system was working its way slowly across the plains. Although the days were getting shorter and the nights were getting much colder, I figured we might have another chance at crossing Lake Michigan. I called both Dan and John to ask if they would like to try again. They both agreed.

On the crisp autumn morning of October 4, 2010, Dan and I once again stood on the shore of Lake Michigan at the Rawley Point Lighthouse in Two Rivers. There was not a cloud in the sky and the sun was already warming the cold 32° morning. There was a slight wind coming from the northwest, yet the seven websites I tracked for water conditions all said the wind and waves would be calm.

At 9 a.m., Dan and I pushed off the west shore of Lake Michigan and headed east across its waters. Our plan was to maintain a paddling pace of 5 mph, taking 5-minute breaks every 2 hours to rest, rehydrate and refuel our bodies. Except for those necessities, Dan and I planned to paddle as hard as we could to ensure a record-breaking end.

Rhythm and timing were a bit of a struggle the first few hours. It was a battle as unexpected side waves would suddenly hit our canoe from different angles, pitching us wildly from side to side and repeatedly forcing us to fight to regain control of our canoe. However, to our pleasant surprise, weather predictions soon proved to be correct. Within a few hours, the waves flattened, leaving us to paddle in calmer water.

Almost everyone can relate to the feeling of working and working and not

DETERMINED DUO. Michael Schnitzka in the bowman seat and Dan Hoffmann behind him attempt to set a world record for canoeing across Lake Michigan.

getting anywhere. It is one of the most frustrating feelings to experience. Since there are no landmarks in the water to give your eyes confirmation that you are actually moving, this feeling was magnified for us while paddling.

Our pace boat with the GPS unit was always the same distance from the canoe, just a few hundred yards ahead of us. Its job was to draw the shortest, straightest line between the two destination points to keep us on track and lead us on the shortest route. Never getting any closer to the support boat while paddling fiercely hour after hour gives you the feeling you have gone nowhere for all your efforts. It's like being on a treadmill going no place fast. It is a mental test as well as physically demanding. Your mind deludes your perceptions of progress and time.

From 15 miles out, we were barely able to eke out the shores of Ludington, Michigan. This indicated we still had 3 hours of paddling to do. I made a conscious effort not to stare at our ending destination for too long. At times, the shore seemed to disappear entirely as we occasionally rose and fell on the swell of small waves—more mind tricks.

The sun was now setting in the west and temperatures were dropping fast. During the last 3 hours of our paddling, the temperature plummeted. Within minutes, it went from a comfortable mid-50s to a very chilling mid-30s.

About 5 miles from shore, we lost our daylight, and with no moon rising, the darkness of night quickly engulfed us. In the darkness, we did not know as we approached shore if we would be met with sand or rocks. We paddled up close and were relieved when we saw the sandy beach. We yelled back to the support boat as the canoe touched terra firma after 11 hours and 22 minutes! We did it! We set a new record!

Dan and I lifted the canoe onto the beach and gave a loud yell followed by a big hug for a job well done. We grabbed our GORE-TEX rain suits for warmth and dashed to the lighthouse. We could see lights on in the windows, so we knocked on the door because a witness was required to confirm our arrival.

We were greeted by a group of people, whom we later learned volunteer in 2-week rotations and give lighthouse tours when needed, in exchange for their room and board. Seeing we were exhausted and cold, they warmed up some sloppy joes and offered us fresh coffee. I think we all know how hot food and coffee offered in kindness will comfort and warm you when cold and exhausted, and this was no exception.

We walked down to the beach with the lighthouse keepers in tow, so they could verify the canoe we used to cross the lake. They bid us farewell as we paddled out a few hundred yards to the support boat. We boarded the support boat, slid the canoe on it, changed into dry clothes and passed out from exhaustion on the floor.

After a short 2-hour nap, I opened my eyes to the most stars I had ever seen. Our location was close to the center of the lake. The nearest light was now 25 miles in any direction. With no moon present, the sky was almost white with stars. It was an amazing sight.

John asked me if I would put our extra 5 gallons of gas in the boat. After I added the gas, I asked John about the gas gauge reading. He mentioned very calmly that it had moved *up* to empty. It took a few moments for that to soak in. I asked if he was kidding, but the look he gave me proved he was not.

We were now 25 miles out, the night was ink black save for the stars, and not a living soul knew we were out there. I didn't ask about the gauge reading again, not needing the knowledge that we could run out of gas out here in the

UNWAVERING WILLPOWER. As a breathtaking sunset reflects off the water, Michael Schnitzka and Dan Hoffmann continue to paddle hard in their attempt to break the world record for the fastest time paddling across Lake Michigan.

dark. The waves continued to grow, making us pitch in all directions. When you are out on large bodies of water, you realize just how fast the curvature of the earth can affect what you see over a long distance. You need to be within 15 miles of shore to see it sitting in a canoe or small boat.

A few hours after adding the gas, we crested a very large wave and I saw the lighthouse light from the very spot we left 17 hours earlier. The waves were so big we were going no faster than the speed it took us to paddle across. Fifteen miles and 3 hours later, we finally cleared the breakwater into port, and I asked John what the gas gauge now read. He joked that it was buried a long time ago, but didn't want to tell Dan and me because he didn't want us to worry.

By 4 a.m., we pulled into Two Rivers Seagull Marina. At this time of the year, there are no boats around, so we had the parking lot to ourselves. In no time, we had the canoe strapped on the car and the support boat hitched up behind us. We dropped Dan off at his car in town, and John and I headed home to Nashotah. I called Dan later in the day and learned he had slept 6 hours in a parking lot, too tired to drive home.

The exhaustion Dan and I felt quickly went away, but the satisfaction at setting the Lake Michigan world record remains. That we achieved it after failing on our first try only makes our success taste that much sweeter. After feeling the pain and agony of failing on the Rhine River, I was almost happy Dan and I failed on our first attempt crossing Lake Michigan. Dan got to experience that these attempts are not easy, that there are many parts that have to come together to even finish—let alone set—a time record. But through hard work and a little bit of luck, we did it.

That's why I always encourage people to keep trying. If you want to accomplish a goal, you can't give up. You don't know if you'll succeed on your first, second or even ninth attempt. But if you keep trying, you're bound to achieve it.

CHAPTER 9

LIGHTNING STRIKES TWICE

"I would rather die of passion than of boredom."
~Émile Zola

Pursuing a dream isn't always easy. It takes imagination, focus, patience and determination. And if it's a long-distance canoe race, it also takes an incredible amount of planning and preparation. And when that race occurs outside the U.S., the planning and prep is multiplied. Besides all the usual necessities—canoe, gear, support team, transportation, food, maps and more—there are additional requirements and regulations that must be followed, depending on the country or countries the race route takes us through.

When Dan and I decided to attempt the world record time for paddling the Rhine River, not only did we want to ensure we followed those regulations, we wanted to be prepared for every eventuality. We had to imagine all the things that could go wrong and have a backup plan ready for each scenario should it occur. And if the backup plan failed, we needed to have an alternate plan to put in place.

For example, one essential item needed for a trip like this is a battery to power our headlight and communication system. We don't have only one. We have three batteries that are continually rotated. While one is in the canoe, the other two are being charged in the support crew vehicle. At every opportunity, a new battery is exchanged to ensure we have fresh power when it's needed. The battery compartment in the canoe is set up for an easy disconnect to not waste the battery's precious power.

The same goes for our drinking water. The support crew van carries a supply of extra drinking water, so they can refill our water bottles every time we see them. If we run out, we carry water purification tablets, so we can drink the same water we are canoeing in. In all my years of marathon racing, I had never needed to use the tablets, which shows that my support crews have done an exemplary job of keeping me supplied with what's needed.

We have always used a marine band radio in the canoe to talk with our support crew on land, but that is sometimes limited by distance and while in river valleys. We don't normally carry cell phones due to the wet environment and rural areas not always having the best service. In addition to the radio, our support crew keeps an eye on our progress by traveling the roads along our route and keeping in visual contact when possible. These are all important safeguards we put in place to ensure we continue the race. For this race, for the first time ever, we carried a GPS tracker. We had set up a tracking system on our website. The GPS transponder sent a signal to our website, allowing anyone interested to follow our progress. While it was helpful to those who viewed our website, it's not the type of device Dan and I could use to help guide our way.

But no matter how much planning you do, no matter how many backup plans you have in place, there are always circumstances beyond your control. At times, these circumstances feel like roadblocks whose only purpose is to test your commitment to reaching your goal.

When you hit one, sometimes you can improvise a solution. Other times, you can turn to a stranger for help. But there are times, despite your best efforts, there is absolutely nothing you can do to overcome a roadblock. Dan and I were going to learn that lesson the hard way.

◆

For almost 30 years, I have paddled Wenonah racing canoes. I feel they are the best built canoes out there. Wenonah has also been very generous to me. The company has provided me with four very expensive boats for various races at no cost. In return, I promoted their product as hard as I could, which I did well. There have been hundreds of articles as well as radio and television interviews about our adventures, and the Wenonah name was always mentioned.

I expected that this trip would be no different. A year earlier, I learned the founder of Wenonah Canoe, Mike Cichanowski, was slowly backing away from running his company and handing it over to his brash son-in-law. I first met Bill Keuper in Madison, Wisconsin, at Canoecopia, the largest canoe and kayak show in the country. It was March 2009 and 2 years before I planned to take another shot at the Rhine River world record. I gave the son-in-law my best sales pitch and asked him if he could help us accomplish the feat. He flat out said, "No." After months of persistence on my part, he finally agreed the company would sponsor us by providing a canoe and shipping it to Frankfurt on the company's dime.

In order for the canoe to arrive in Germany in time for our race, it had to be ready to go at the Wenonah factory no later than December 1, 2010. When I arrived at the factory that December day, employees from the plant came out to see the 19-foot Kevlar canoe adorned with the Wenonah name. The Itasca, as it's

START OF THE RHINE RIVER. Dan Hoffmann and Michael Schnitzka wave to onlookers as they begin the race in Chur, Switzerland.

called, is a tripping canoe with high sides and big volume, but incredibly light. It could handle any water conditions the Rhine River would throw at us. It was fully wired for sound and lights and covered with a skintight tarp from Harken, a manufacturer of sailboat hardware and accessories based in Pewaukee, Wisconsin. The canoe looked beautiful.

The front desk person at Wenonah handed me some paperwork to sign— along with a bill for $1,000 for shipping the canoe to Germany. I was shocked! That wasn't the deal we'd agreed upon months earlier! I asked to speak to the son-in-law. When he came out, he simply stated that he had changed his mind. I had two choices: pay the shipping or find another sponsor to provide a canoe. With the canoe race only months away, what choice did I have? He had me over a barrel. I paid the bill with my credit card and left. I wasn't happy with the turn of events, but I'd cleared what I hoped was the only roadblock we'd encounter on our endeavor.

◆

On April 14, 2011, Dan and I, along with Mike Mlynarski, my longtime support crew chief, and Rick Stoddard, a new addition to the team, landed in Frankfurt. Our third support crew member would arrive the next day. We took a cab to the rental agency to pick up the camper we had reserved, then drove to the retail canoe store that was storing our boat. We loaded up the canoe and headed south toward Chur, where our race would begin. It was almost a full day's drive to get there, and we took advantage of the route to show Dan and our support crew the rapids as well as the locks and dams we would encounter. When we reached Chur, we settled in for the night at a campground across the street from the race's starting point.

The next day, I set off for the train station to meet Dan's brother, Tom Hoffmann, the third member of our support crew. On my way, I bumped into Corrado Filipponi, the Swiss travel photojournalist who had set the Rhine River world record the previous year with a time of 7 days, 10 hours, 16 minutes. I had been in contact with him via email, and he had written that he would try to be there when Dan and I began our race. I was delighted when Corrado said not only would he be there, but so would most of the support crew that helped him achieve his record time.

The weather was below freezing when Dan and I woke up before sunrise the next morning. We took the last hot showers we'd get for quite some time and headed to the race start. A small crowd, including Corrado, had gathered to see us off. At 7 a.m., the clock started, and Dan and I pushed off to set the world record on the Rhine River. When Bill and I set the time record for the 2,348-mile Mississippi River race, we averaged 4.1 mph. The Rhine is 720 miles long and has a much faster current, so I felt we could average 5 mph. That meant we should finish in exactly 6 days.

The plan was for our support crew to follow us along the banks of the Rhine to take pictures and keep an eye on us. The river starts in a lovely scenic area in the Swiss Alps. In the first 50 miles, the river drops 500 feet in elevation, allowing us to maintain a much higher average speed than our goal. We'd been paddling a few hours when we realized we hadn't glimpsed our support crew since the start. But we did see Corrado and his support crew riding bicycles on paths on each side of the river, following our progress.

Dan and I expected to meet our support crew to resupply before entering the section of river that dumps into Lake Constance, a glacial body of water that is one of Europe's largest. After 10 hours of paddling, we arrived at the meeting spot to get fresh supplies. The only person there was a member of

BOW OUT OF THE WATER. A fast current and drop in elevation create choppy waters on the Rhine River for the paddlers. Their flat-water racing canoe is not meant for those conditions.

Corrado's crew. It put a shiver down my spine when he said he had not seen our support crew all day. We should have seen them dozens of times by this point, and we had not seen them since the beginning.

Lake Constance is approximately 25 miles long by 5 miles wide and shallow, so if it's windy, there are very large waves to contend with. Because there was no wind—similar to my 2007 attempt—I expected we wouldn't have problems. Dan and I decided not to wait for the crew or for the weather to change, and we paddled out into the large lake. We were very low on drinking water, so when canoeing along its southern shoreline, we spotted a boat marina. We stopped and ran into the men's bathroom to fill our nearly empty water containers.

With the sun slowly setting, we continued paddling west along the southern shore, listening to music on our headsets. We were about 800 yards offshore when Dan abruptly stopped because he thought he heard people calling our names. Sure enough, our support crew was at another marina 5 miles west of our last stop. They were yelling our names to catch our attention. We gladly

CALM CONDITIONS. Despite being low on food and water, the canoeists decide to take advantage of the lack of wind and start paddling across Lake Constance, rather than wait for their support crew to arrive to resupply them.

paddled in to meet them, because we were now out of food and maps, and we needed a fresh battery.

Crew Chief Mike explained the reason we hadn't seen them all day—the brand-new camper trailer we had rented hit a bump in the road, damaging the front right wheel bearing and making the vehicle undrivable. He had been trying to reach the rental agency for a replacement, but its office was closed on the weekend. Our crew was exploring other transportation options, but they made it clear the situation could become a roadblock to finishing the race. There was nothing Dan and I could do but hope our crew found a way to overcome this obstacle.

We loaded up extra food and water in case we wouldn't see them for a while and continued on our journey. We were 12 hours into the race at this time, and our goal was to paddle for 48 hours before we took a sleep break. Night came on quickly, and our planned full moon rose to give us a glorious paddle across Lake Constance.

It's hard to describe certain memories of these adventure races. Sometimes, a song on the radio will jog my thoughts to a time on the water. Sometimes, it's a smell. Other times, it might be catching sight of something that I saw while paddling. My memory of that night paddling is wonderful.

As the light slowly faded and night approached, my eyes adjusted, allowing me to see every detail even better. If I close my eyes right now, I can place myself in the canoe, silently paddling along and hearing the gentle slap of our paddles hitting the smooth surface of the water. I had taken off my headphones to soak in all that I could of my breathtaking surroundings. Dan and I went from marveling at the beautiful Swiss Alps, with gorgeous expensive homes on shore in the bright sunshine, to paddling in the darkness, waiting for the full moon to rise and provide more light.

The cloudless night was amazing. Most people don't take the time to watch the moon rise like the sun. It's something you really need to see. The moon looked huge reflecting off the placid lake. The water was so clear that Dan and I could see the lake bottom, 20 feet down, by moonlight. That night gave me an amazing memory I will carry with me for the rest of my life.

Around midnight, we paddled into the large city of Konstanz, where the Rhine water returns to river form, never again to been seen a different way. The voice of a member of our support crew crackled on the radio telling us the crew was just ahead at another marina. When we arrived, Mike told us the rental agency had not returned any of his multiple messages, and our crew was doing the best they could. He gave us extra food and water—in fact, much more than normal. That was the first time that had ever happened, and I knew Mike was silently telling me things were really bad. I kept these worried thoughts from my paddling partner, and we continued on through the night.

The sun was coming up as Dan and I entered the town of Schaffhausen, Switzerland. We were only 24 hours into the race, yet despite all our problems, we were 6 hours ahead of schedule. The portage in Schaffhausen is by far the longest one at 2-1/2 miles long. The Rhine Falls, a large waterfall, is located there. We took out our canoe where boat traffic is stopped, more than a mile before the falls.

Since the beginning of the race, we had carried a set of portage wheels in the canoe. This small device cradles your canoe, allowing you to pick up one end and walk, pulling the canoe behind you when portaging. Portage wheels are allowed in a race like this but must be carried in the canoe from the start, never being handed back to the support crew and retrieved. The downside to

LATE-NIGHT RENDEZVOUS. Support crew members Mike Mlynarski and Tom Hoffmann watch Dan Hoffmann adjust his backrest at a marina near Konstanz.

having them is that on a difficult portage where the wheels cannot be used, they become unneeded weight you must carry.

They were a godsend on the long portage in Schaffhausen. Yet it must have been an interesting sight to see two men pulling a canoe on wheels through the middle of this small town at sunrise.

We found our support crew halfway through the long walk, but they had no news about replacing our broken support vehicle. So we again loaded up our canoe with extra supplies and put in the river just below the falls.

The weather turned very warm, so Dan and I drank a lot of water to keep hydrated as we paddled. Unlike the lake with its marinas, there were no places along the river to stop for fresh water. When we finished our supply, we turned to our backup plan. We refilled our containers with river water, and for the first time ever in an adventure race, I used purification tablets to make it safe to drink.

By 2 p.m. on the second day of our race, we had eaten all of our food, and the battery for our communication system was dead. We urgently needed to meet up with our support crew to resupply. We had our trusty GPS transponder in the boat and a quick check showed the light was still blinking. The support

HANDY PORTAGE WHEELS. A set of wheels attached to the stern of the boat helps Dan Hoffmann and Michael Schnitzka transport the canoe during long portages, like this one in Schaffhausen, Switzerland.

crew could go online and see where we were at any time, but the reverse was not the case. They could be just around the corner and we wouldn't know. I was doing the best I could to keep up our spirits, but I knew this was not a good sign.

This next section of the Rhine is very dangerous. There are a lot of big dams that create whirlpools and turbulent water. Just after the town of Laufenburg, Switzerland, we reached another dam at sunset. Since we were still way ahead of schedule, I told Dan we needed to sit and wait for our support group to catch up to us. I knew the support crew was tracking us via the GPS unit in our canoe, and I was confident they would find us. It would be difficult for us to navigate the river in the dark without our headlight, so it was safer to stay put. We had now paddled 36 hours without sleep, and our food and water intake was not what we needed to keep up this fast pace.

We were still high in altitude, and the temperature was dropping fast. Dan and I were dressed for the warmer days in light windbreaker tops and bottoms, so we quickly felt the chill. While we waited for our crew, we scouted out the area and found a public park near the dam. There, we spotted a large pile of wood and a fire pit. But we didn't have any matches to start a fire. And why would we? We expected the support crew would always be there for us. Not this time. Dan walked a half-mile into town to a gas station, where he used broken German to ask for a pack of matches.

When he returned, we built a fire and huddled near it for warmth. It helped, but with the temperature about 32°, it was not enough. We were still freezing, so we removed the Harken cover from our canoe and wrapped it around us to retain our body heat. I've gone winter camping in my youth, but nothing I have experienced in my life prepared me for the cold I felt that night.

Dan and I were chilled to the bone, tired and hungry, and our support crew was nowhere in sight. I told Dan that we only had a few more hours left to be able to continue on our race, but that window was closing fast. We'd managed to build a fire and find drinking water at the park, so we were hopeful we could continue, but we still had nothing to eat.

About 2 a.m., 7 hours after we'd arrived at the dam, Corrado had switched from his bicycle to his car and found us in the park. He had been following our progress from the beginning and knew something was wrong when our signal had stopped moving. He'd heard our support vehicle had encountered problems, and he promised to do his best to contact our crew with our whereabouts. We discussed our options, and I decided to stay put and wait for our crew to show up. I was so confident that our crew would find us shortly that I never thought to ask him for food. That was a mistake.

After he left, it took me a few minutes to realize our friends, family and sponsors back home were likely also wondering why our tracking beacon stopped moving on the website. I found out when we got back home, most had feared the worst—that we had capsized and drowned. Only after Corrado reached our support crew did everyone find out we were fine...just cold, tired and hungry.

When the sun finally came up, we left our canoe hidden behind some bushes near the river and walked to town. Dan and I were exhausted. I think between us we got a combined hour of sleep that night. We found the city

> *"I found out when we got back home, most had feared the worst— that we had capsized and drowned."*

tourism bureau office and explained our circumstances. The staff spoke perfect English and kindly allowed us to send emails to our families and our support crew to tell them where we were and that we were OK. A woman in the office was particularly nice, handing us money out of her purse, so we could buy food to eat.

Many people have asked me why we didn't have matches or money in our canoe. I sometimes come back asking, "Why didn't we bring a favorite pillow or perhaps a book to read in case we had to stop?" In all the years of racing, I had never been so stranded or felt so helpless. You just cannot plan for all the potential problems that might occur. And the thought of needing matches or currency would never have been on my list—ever.

At this point, we were several hours behind schedule, and I didn't see a way we could make up that time. We were not even halfway through the race when we had to admit defeat. I couldn't believe it, but lightning had struck twice. I had failed twice on the Rhine River. Now, it was all about getting the team back together to make our way home.

Dan, of course, was not happy with the outcome. This was the second failure for me on the Rhine and I accepted it. I told Dan to be proud of what we had done to this point. From the beginning, this had not gone well, but we pushed on and adapted. When something totally out of your control ends your race, you just have to say, "It wasn't meant to be."

Later that afternoon, Dan and I were waiting back at the park when Corrado pulled up in his car. He said our support crew was trying to get our vehicle fixed at a truck dealership 70 miles away. He offered to drive us there, so we hid our canoe behind a storage shed at the park and jumped into Corrado's car.

When we arrived at the dealership, we were greeted with the very long faces of our support crew. The entire time during the race, they knew we were way ahead of schedule and there was a distinct possibility of smashing the existing record. And now it was all over. There was nothing left to do but pack up and go home with our tails between our legs. We were told a new RV was on its way down from Frankfurt, but it was not going to arrive for hours. So we all walked down to a local pub, and I enjoyed my first beer in 6 months.

As a side note to those contemplating an attempt like this, do it during the week. Not many things are open on the weekends in some countries, including

NO CRYING IN YOUR BEER. At Munich's famous Hofbräuhaus, Michael Schnitzka and Mike Mlynarski toast to a valiant attempt at breaking the world speed record paddling the Rhine River.

RV dealerships that promise to come to the rescue right away if there are any problems with your vehicle. They don't tell you the office is closed on the weekend, and if you have problems, you'll have to wait to give them a call on Monday. Our final roadblock was something we could not control: bad timing. If the problem had occurred during the week when the agency was open, we'd have been able to continue the race.

———◆———

We spent the next week traveling through southern Germany, doing some sightseeing while we waited for our plane ride home. We took a gondola ride up to the snowcapped Zugspitze Mountain, the highest point in Germany. Then, it was off to Berchtesgaden, the site of Hitler's Eagle's Nest.

We spent the nights sleeping in our camper in ALDI grocery store parking lots. I had done some research before leaving the U.S. and learned ALDI was a place wayward campers could go to rest and the police would leave them be. It must've been funny to see five guys sitting around in the middle of a parking lot as the sun went down. But that's what we did.

And, of course, a visit to Germany isn't complete without stopping in Munich to have a beer at the Hofbräuhaus. It was Easter weekend and we were working our way back to Frankfurt to drop off the replacement RV. Even the tourist attractions were closed, so we spent most of those days at waysides, just killing time. We got a hotel room near the airport the night before we left, so everyone could take hot showers and sleep in beds instead of cramped areas in the RV.

In the morning, we drove to the airport. Dan planned to stay in the country awhile to do some rock climbing, so it was his job to return the RV. We had done a spectacular job cleaning the vehicle—a requirement of the rental agreement. Unfortunately, the RV dealer thought our job was lacking, so Dan had to clean for hours while the rest of us enjoyed a movie and cocktails at 30,000 feet.

We arranged for Corrado to pick up our canoe from the park. About a month later, he found someone to buy it, and we split the money with him for helping us.

A few weeks after my return, Dan called to say he was back home too. He thanked me for the opportunity and experience of chasing a world record on one of the most historic rivers in the world. In turn, I thanked him for allowing me one more chance to try to cross off an item on my bucket list.

When telling the story of paddling the Rhine River two times, I often use the word *failure*. Most people shrug it off and say I should be proud to even have attempted it once, let alone twice. I just cannot accept that, and I know I will be haunted until my dying days for not getting to Rotterdam in the Netherlands to dip my toes in the cold waters of the North Sea.

CHAPTER 10

FROM PADDLE TO PEDAL

"Do not fear failure but rather fear not trying."
~Roy T. Bennett

June 21, 2015

It's 120°, and the blazing sun continues to beat down on me as I head north on Arizona's State Road 95. It's halfway into the second day of the 3,000-mile Race Across America, and I've been sidelined by a flat rear tire. My cycling shoes *clip-clop* on the scorching asphalt as I walk my bike along the race route.

Usually, my support crew is in a van right behind me. If they had been, they would have replaced the flat tire and got me back on the road in minutes. But I'm all alone. The crew left me to drive my race partner, who has been incapacitated by the heat, to the time station in Parker, Arizona, where our RV awaits. They hope a cool shower and a change of atmosphere will revive him so he can race again.

It's been over an hour since I last saw them, and I'm worried. I'm in rough shape. I have not slept a minute since the race started 24 hours ago. I've choked down every drop of steamy water in my two water bottles in an effort to keep dehydration at bay, but now they're bone dry.

I'm determined to finish this race. I refuse to fail. But I can't finish it if I don't get out of this heat—soon. As I survey the horizon, anticipating the appearance of the support van, my mind flashes back to 2 years earlier when I failed to finish canoeing the length of the Rhine River for a second time.

———◆———

I came home from Europe with my tail between my legs and decided to retire from ultramarathon racing. But I couldn't go through with it. For some reason, I have this little flame that's always burning inside of me, a yearning to seek out a new goal to achieve.

So I called up my old canoe partner, Bill Perdzock, and asked if he would like to bike in the RAAM, the world's toughest bike race. While we were too old to consider going after the speed record, as a two-man team, maybe we could set a new time in the 50 and older category. It took about 3 seconds for Bill to say, "Hell, no!"

His refusal didn't deter me. I racked my brain to think of an alternate teammate. I remembered my cousin Dave Traxel was into bicycle racing. He

> *"I have this little flame that's always burning inside of me, a yearning to seek out a new goal to achieve."*

was just 2 years older than me and very athletic. In his senior year of high school, he was one of the fastest men in the state at the 100- and 200-yard dash. I gave him a call, and we sat down for a few hours to discuss the race.

Dave was typically doing 30- to 50-mile races and had not even tried a 100-mile bicycle race. When he agreed to do this 3,000-mile race with me, I knew he had a lot of training ahead. Our goal for the race was to bike an average of 18 mph. If we did that, we estimated it would take 7 days to complete the race if one of us was always biking. To be prepared for that kind of grueling activity, our training would have to get us in tip-top shape. It would not only be physical training, but mental training—preparing his mind to handle the extreme highs and lows of an ultramarathon sport. I knew it was a big gamble, but we had 2 years to get ready, I reasoned.

A long and difficult race like the RAAM requires top-of-the-line equipment. Dave told me his girlfriend had a connection to a large bicycle manufacturer. After a few phone calls and meetings, Jamis Bicycles agreed to sponsor us, giving both of us a $2,400 carbon fiber bicycle. The model chosen for the RAAM was the Jamis Xenith Endura Comp, which weighed in at a very light 19 pounds. Bicycles, like canoes, come in all shapes and sizes. This model was designed for long-distance bicycling, so it had a much taller head tube and a longer frame to make the ride more comfortable. And without a doubt, the most important thing on the bicycle was the seat. After much research, we decided on an all-leather Brooks saddle. Now, one would think a leather seat with no padding would be uncomfortable, but imagine a worn-in baseball glove after a season of catching balls. Dave and I knew the seat would be hard as a rock in the beginning, but super-soft come race time.

Back in the day, I had competed in quite a few canoe triathlons, so I was familiar with putting miles on a bicycle. But it had been years since I spent any time in the saddle, and I knew I had a lot of work to do just to catch up to Dave.

Dave joined the health club where I was a member so we could train together. I showed him the exercises he needed to do—not just biking, but working on strengthening his core. I also helped him change his diet, so he was consuming the best fuel for his body. Every fiber in your body must be in shape to participate in a demanding bicycle race like this, even your mind. We talked about how punishing the race would be, and that willpower and determination were the things that would get us through it. And while I can train athletes to be physically tough, I can't train them to be mentally tough.

Despite 2 years of training, the gamble I took is not paying off. Dave has struggled from the get-go. First, I think he was overwhelmed by the scope of the race. The starting line at Oceanside Pier, California, was crowded with hundreds of competitors, including two-, four- and eight-person relay teams. There were even international teams with their own film crews. Plus, there were thousands more people cheering on teams, and filming or photographing the event. I don't think he had realized what a big deal the race was.

Racers are queued at the starting line and begin pedaling as soon as their names are announced over a loudspeaker. Even though only one person at a time bikes for each relay team, the beginning of the race allows all team members to start together. The route goes along the beach for a few hundred yards— elevation less than 50 feet—then it follows a maze of rural residential roads, slowly climbing the mountains in the San Diego area. After the first 5 miles of the race, everyone on a team must pull off the race route except one.

After Dave pulled off, I did the next 15 miles alone. Then Dave and I began the process of switching riders, which we did when we got tired and needed a break. We took turns biking 30-minute periods, and he caught on quickly to the procedures we'd agreed upon for working with our support crew and taking turns biking.

We had a brand-new support crew, which consisted of Dave Allen, Mike Walker, Tom Traxel (Dave's brother), Ellen Holly and Colleen Robson. Two crew members would drive the support van that followed closely behind the racer. The van driver's job was to keep a close but safe distance behind the biker to protect him from traffic. The other crew member in the vehicle helped with navigation, reading maps and alerting the driver to what was coming up next.

The three remaining members were in a huge recreational vehicle that we called the Mothership. It was usually ahead of us, waiting at one of the more

AND THEY'RE OFF! Dave Traxel and Michael Schnitzka pedal across the 2015 RAAM starting line in Oceanside, California.

than 50 time stations along the route. Those crew members would monitor the race route, buy necessary supplies, help with food prep and grab some shut-eye before it was their turn to man the support van.

The plan was for Dave Traxel or me to always be biking during the trip. While Dave biked, I rested in the support van and vice versa. There was never a time we would be in the Mothership. We had no reason to be there, because the support van held all the supplies and equipment we needed.

When it was time for us to switch places, we had a signal—a few taps to the head—to alert the support crew in the van. If I was biking, I would tap my head with my hand to indicate I was close to being done. That signal meant the support crew should wake Dave, fill his water bottles and get him ready to go.

The next time I tapped my head, probably 10 minutes after the first, it meant the van should pass me by 300 to 400 yards, then pull over. The support crew would take Dave's bike off the rack on the van and put fresh water bottles on it, so Dave could just hop on. When I caught up to the van, I had to pass Dave on his bike by one length before he could start biking. It's sort of like passing the baton in relay race at a track meet. And that's how a two-man team hops and skips across the country for this race.

MOBILE MONITOR. The team's support van is stocked with race provisions, spare equipment and a mattress where one racer can rest while the other bikes. The van follows closely behind the racer to protect him from traffic along the route.

When the route hit State Route 76 in Rincon, the ascent got steeper as it climbed Palomar Mountain. The first day's highest point was near Ranchita—elevation more than 4,000 feet. It was also the most exciting part of the day, because it was the beginning of "The Glass Elevator"—a 9-mile, 3,000-plus-foot descent to the floor of the Anza-Borrego Desert with spectacular views.

It was Dave's first adventure race, and we had scheduled our shifts so that he would take his bicycle down this wild ride. But the heat had done a number on him, and he'd shortened his shifts, so our schedule was off track and I ended up riding "The Glass Elevator." What an amazing experience!

At the top of the run, the temperature was about 80°. I picked up speed as I descended, going 45 to 60 miles per hour. You would expect the wind to cool you down going that fast, but every curve I took racing down to the desert got hotter and hotter. By the time I reached the desert floor, the temperature was well over 110°, but it felt like I was standing in front of a 500° oven with its door open.

Because the race is so congested in the beginning, none of the racers have met up with their RVs yet. Our crew in the Mothership, like the support crews in RVs for all the other racers, had been waiting all day in the little California

THE RACE ACROSS AMERICA (RAAM) is a 3,000-mile cross-country ultramarathon—the world's toughest bicycle race, tougher than the Tour de France.

town of Borrego Springs for the racers to arrive. The sun was slowly setting in the west when Dave and I, along with our support van, reached the RV.

Dave and I resupplied our support van for the first time, and our support crew rotated. We had a fresh driver, Mike Walker, and map reader, Colleen Robson. By this time, I had been on the bicycle about an hour and was thinking of taking a break. But Dave said he was not quite rested enough, so I kept pedaling as we headed southeast into the desert darkness toward Brawley, 57 miles away.

Dave and I continued to switch biking every 30 minutes or so, giving each other a rest because the temperature was still 85° in the middle of the night. Our speed was down, lower than what we wanted, but we planned to make up the time later.

After Time Station No. 2 in Brawley, the route followed California State Route 78 straight east. It was still nighttime when I biked through the North Algodones Dunes Wilderness Area, and my headlight picked up some reflective material about a mile in front of me. I couldn't imagine what it was. I was in the middle of sand dunes with no people or towns in sight. As I pedaled, I tried to figure out what these tall reflective objects were. I looked to my right, and way off in the distance, I saw a light coming my way. It was slowly getting closer to me as I got closer to the reflective objects. Then it clicked—those objects were safety gates at a railroad crossing. And closing in quickly from the right was a train.

My tired brain calculated whether I could reach the crossing before the train arrived. It determined I would lose the race with the train if I didn't pick up my speed. I quickly jumped out of my seat, kicked it into a bigger gear and started sprinting toward the reflective gates. Sprinting for more than a mile in that heat was an ordeal, and just before I reached the crossing, the gates came down. A train came flying by, and I had no choice but to stand there and watch it.

My support van pulled up next to me and rolled down the windows, and we all started laughing. Even my partner, Dave, who was resting in the back of the van, laughed at how hard I had just worked for nothing. About the time I figured out it was a train coming, so did they. They had been cheering me on in the van, hoping I'd make it across the tracks before the train arrived. Now, we all had to wait—it seemed like 20 minutes—for this incredibly long train to pass by before we could continue the race.

Dave and I continued to take turns biking to Time Station No. 3 in Blythe.

From there, we headed north on California State Route 95, which runs along the Colorado River. South of Vidal, California, the route took a slight jog east, and we crossed into Arizona, on our way to Time Station No. 4 in a town called Parker.

It's at this point in the blistering race that things got really interesting. When Dave signaled that he needed to rest, we agreed the support van would drive him ahead to our RV, which was waiting at Time Station No. 4. That decision brought me to my current circumstances: walking my broken-down bike and *clip-clopping* in my cycling shoes toward Parker.

It's been over an hour since I last saw my support crew, and I'm exhausted, incredibly hot and unbelievably thirsty. I estimate I've walked 4 miles and have 3 miles to go to meet up with my crew. As I scan the horizon, I glimpse movement—there's a vehicle coming toward me. As it approaches, I recognize the white support van, and as it gets closer yet, I see that Dave Allen is driving. When he reaches me, he circles the van behind me and gives me a worried look that asks, "Why are you walking?"

I point down to the popped back tire, and he quickly figures it out. He jumps out of the van and grabs my partner's bicycle off the top. My cousin Dave gets out of the van and onto his bike. He's going to pedal the 3 miles to the RV. Dave

IN THE HOT SEAT. Brutal desert temperatures hamper the progress of numerous RAAM racers, including the two-man team of Michael Schnitzka (above) and Dave Traxel.

Allen throws my bicycle on the van, and he and I race off, leaving my partner alone for the first time.

We get to Time Station No. 4, and Dave Allen removes one of the two spare tires we carry on top of the van for just such an event. Dave is very knowledgeable with bicycle mechanics. In only a minute, he removes the flat, installs the spare, centers the wheel in the frame, cinches the chain around the gears and has my bike ready to go.

While we wait for my partner to arrive, I sit in the front seat of the support van, cranking the air-conditioning so the blessedly cool air blows directly on me. After walking 4 miles in 120° heat, I seriously need to chill out. I'm there resting when my partner gets into the van.

Not wasting a second, I say, "Dave, you gotta keep going!"

"I'm really hot and I need to take a break," he replies.

After biking only 3 miles? The adrenaline kicks in and compels me to get out of the van. I'm so angry, it's a surprise I can even refill my water bottles from the cooler in the back of van. All five members of the support crew are now standing around me.

"Get Dave ready," I tell them. "I'm going to set my watch for 30 minutes. And at 30, I'm done. And I'm done for a while." I know my body, and my core temperature has been creeping up toward the danger zone. I have maybe 30 minutes left in me before I need a very long rest. I take a quick look at the topographical maps. They show hills coming up, so it's going to be a steady climb to the mountains I can see out in the distance. I'll be biking uphill in the 120° dry, desert heat with no wind and no clouds. It's going to be brutal. But that's not going to stop me.

I reset the timer on my bicycle for 30 minutes and started pedaling. I try to take a few gulps from my water bottle, but I feel a little wobbly. The heat has really taken a toll on me. I've been an ultramarathon athlete since 1984, and I have never felt this dizzy. I start weaving a bit on the bike, and I'm very aware that I'm not hitting on all cylinders. I feel like I'm drunk, and it's a struggle to do simple things, like stay on the road and keep my balance.

I have a little rearview mirror on my helmet so I can see behind me, and I'm anxiously waiting for the white support van to come into view. I keep pedaling. It's been 20 minutes, and there's still no sign of it. I take one of the bottles and soak the front of my thighs, then spray the rest of the water down my helmet and back. I keep going. At 25 minutes, I'm thinking, "Damn it! Why aren't they here? I shouldn't be out here alone. They should be right behind me!" I'm on a two-lane interstate, and semitrucks are passing me just a few feet to my left.

As the seconds pass, I start to get worried, imagining all the things that could have happened since I left the crew. At 28 minutes, I see a white dot in my mirror, which slowly gets bigger. When I see bicycle tires on top, I know it's the support van. As the timer on my bike beeps 30 minutes, I pull over and the van is right there.

I haven't unclipped my shoes from the bike pedals when Mike Walker, a former paramedic, gets out of the van and comes over. He notices that my eyes are sort of wiggling, going back and forth, left to right.

"I'm not feeling well," I tell him.

"You don't look well," he replies.

He urges me to get off my bike and into the front passenger seat of the van. Ellen Holly jumps out of the seat and I hop in. I turn up the air-conditioning to full blast, angle the vents toward me and take off my helmet. It's the most heavenly feeling to just sit there with the rush of cold air blowing on me.

Mike opens my door and puts a digital thermometer in my mouth. Almost instantly it beeps. He looks at the reading and says, "104. You're done for a while. I'll be right back."

He shuts the door and I'm so damned hot, I don't want to do anything but rest my head on the dash and try to absorb the cold air. My eyes are closed when the door opens again. Seconds later, Mike drops an ice-cold, soaking wet towel across my back, and I feel like I've been electrically shocked! It's such a jolt to my system, I gasp for breath and my whole body tenses up and goes, *Whoa!* It sounds odd, but it takes a few seconds for me to realize I'm not being burned and that the wet towel is, in fact, freezing cold. I'm amazed I don't have a heart attack.

Mike apologizes for not warning me and explains that I was within minutes of heatstroke, and he felt the best option for quickly reducing my body temperature was a bath towel soaked in a cooler full of ice water. I know he's right. If I don't get cooled down fast, I'm going to pass out, so I sit there with the icy-cold, wet towel around my shoulders.

"It's your turn to get on the bike," I say to my partner, Dave, who's still resting on a mattress in the back of the van. "The meter's running. Just go!" Our goal was to never stop moving. It's critical not to stop. Even if you're going only 5 mph, it's better than going 0 mph. You gotta keep moving.

"I'm too hot to do anything more," Dave says.

"You're not as hot as me," I reply angrily. My body temp is going down, but my rage meter is going up. "You have to get out and continue the race!" I tell him. "The whole race is on you right now. It's on your shoulders. Because I need a break. I really need to cool down, hydrate and eat something. If you don't get out there, the race is over, because I can't go anymore for quite some time."

He pauses for a second and then says, "I can't. I'm done."

That's it.

Mike and Ellen agree with the decision to quit the race, but I don't. You see, I don't tap out. I'll pass out before I tap out. That's just part of ultramarathon races. Going in, you know it's going to suck. And you deal with it. You embrace the suck. If the RAAM were easy, everyone would do it. There's a reason it's called the world's toughest bicycle race. It's going to suck. When it does, you

> "*Going in, you know it's going to suck. And you deal with it. You embrace the suck.*"

overcome it. You push through it. When every fiber in your body is saying, *Why are you doing this? You really should stop*, that's when you keep going. You get over that hump and continue on.

The Mothership hasn't left Parker, so we put my bike on top of the van, turn around and head back to the time station there. As I cool down during the drive, I start to do the math. I know we are behind, but by how much? And what's ahead on the route? Maybe the race isn't over for us. Maybe we call this a time-out. The RAAM is a really long race. It's going to take 8 or 9 days maybe. What's an hour or two of not moving if it means we can finish? We haven't notified race officials that our team is done, so we can still do this.

When we reach Parker, I stay in the van and grab the RAAM route book. I open it to our current location and review the route ahead of us, checking the elevation. It's going to be uphill for a bit. I flip through the next few pages. Hmm… When is it going to get flat? I keep turning page after page after page. And the elevation keeps going up and up and up to the Rockies. Oh, my God.

Can we do it? Mentally, I'm fine. Physically, I'm a little hurt. But I can cool down, hydrate, eat something and get back on the bike. I can suck it up. But not Dave. He isn't in the right frame of mind to be able to handle the brutality of it. Although I try, I can't change his mind no matter what I say.

We made it roughly 300 miles into a 3,000-mile bicycle race. Once again, I feel the sting of not accomplishing a goal. I can't describe the crushing feeling after putting so much time, energy and money into something and not even getting close to the finish line.

Though it doesn't ease the sting, I later learn half of the solo and two-man teams didn't make it through this part of the route either. They tapped out. The teams that did get through this section took desperate measures. Some support crews wrapped their racers in ice in imaginative ways. Some bought women's sports bras from a store in the area for their racers to wear, then filled the bras with ice packs to keep the racers' hearts, lungs and core cool. Unfortunately, we never got to that point. Would measures like that have made the difference? I'll never know.

◆

After my failure on the RAAM, I came home with my tail between my legs again. I sat down and pondered the next adventures I wanted to pursue. They were different from the ones I'd already accomplished. You see, after training and competing in long-distance endurance events for 30 years, my body had taken quite the abuse. To date, I have had surgery on my left knee, my back (a bulging disk), both shoulders twice and a broken collarbone. I also had malignant skin cancer removed. There comes a time in everyone's life when the mind is willing but the body is weak. My time had come.

For some reason, I have always been drawn to the water. Over the past few years, I have sailed on Lake Michigan on a competitive racing team. I find extreme joy in getting something to move fast over water without a motor. One of my longtime dreams is to retire on a catamaran sailboat and sail the world. To do so will require a lot of work and patience.

I need to earn my light, medium and heavy wind certifications through the American Sailing Association. I would also like to get my captain's license. While it's not needed to live on a sailboat, it would allow me to teach sailing and have paying customers aboard my vessel. To be able to work on the catamaran's two motors, I would need to take classes in diesel mechanics.

My goal in life, as I hope it is for you, is always to get in as much as I can. Come my untimely demise, I want to know I left nothing on the table. I gave it my all and my best. You should aim to do the same, because…

Tomorrow is promised to no one.

SPORTS-RELATED EXPERIENCE

World Record Holder – canoeing Mississippi River, fastest time

World Record Holder – canoeing Wisconsin River, fastest time

World Record Holder – crossing Lake Michigan by canoe, fastest time

Motivational Speaker

Triathlete

Adventure Racer

20,000+ miles paddling experience

Race Across America competitor

Named one of "12 of the City's Most Fascinating Men," *M Milwaukee's
    Lifestyle Magazine*, March 2011

Trainer for competitors in ultramarathon sports

Dietary consultant for ultramarathon athletes

U.S. Army veteran

WORK-RELATED INFORMATION

New business development professional

25+ years cold calling experience

Corporate sales trainer

Non-interest fee income expert

Salesman to and trainer for employees at companies including:

- MarineMax, the world's largest recreational boat dealership company
- Bass Pro Shops, outdoor recreation retailer
- SkipperBud's, boat dealership
- Gander Mountain, outdoor gear retailer
- Numerous billion dollar+ asset-sized financial institutions

Licenses held:

Life, Health, Property, Casualty

Previous Sponsor Websites

Wenonah Canoe (handcrafted canoes)	*wenonah.com*
Budget Rent a Car (car rental agency)	*budget.com*
Hofbräu München (traditional Munich brewery)	*hofbraeu-muenchen.de*
Potawatomi Hotel & Casino	*paysbig.com*
Noodles & Company (franchise)	*truecoffeeroasters.com*
Jamis Bikes (road and mountain bikes)	*jamisbikes.com*
Kialoa Paddles (outrigger, stand up and other paddles)	*kialoa.com*
Harken (sailboat hardware and accessories)	*harken.com*
Laacke & Joys (outdoor outfitter)	*ljoutdoors.com*
BadgerMax (sports drinks)	*badgermax.com*
Mini Spotlights (LED lighting)	*minispotlight.com*
Remy Battery (batteries and power accessories)	*remybattery.com*
Batteries Plus Bulbs (batteries, light bulbs and repair)	*batteriesplus.com*
Raymarine (marine electronics)	*raymarine.com*
Quad/Graphics (print and media solutions provider)	*qg.com*

MAN OF INTRIGUE. Michael Schnitkza was featured in the article "12 of the City's Most Fascinating Men" in the March 2011 edition of *M Milwaukee's Lifestyle Magazine.*

Mike Schnitzka holds the Guinness Book of World Records title for canoeing the Mississippi River and is the record holder for canoeing the Wisconsin River and crossing Lake Michigan. The Nashotah resident is currently training to race in the Conquer the Rhine, a world-record canoe race to take place on the Rhine River in Germany this April.

mind over water

Mike Schnitzka | Canoeing Extremist

Mike Schnitzka has one more mountain to climb — make that one more river to paddle.

On April 16, he and Dan Hoffmann will attempt to break the world speed record on the Rhine River in Europe. It's been Schnitzka's goal since 1989. That's the year he and long-time race partner Bill Perdzock set the record for canoeing 2,348 miles on the Mississippi River and the year the British Royal Airforce Canoe Team set the record for canoeing the 720-mile Rhine. "What record do you think made the Guiness Book of World Records?" Schnitza says. "We canoed three times farther and were never mentioned."

He and Perdzock attempted to break the record in 2007, but were stopped by their support crew after they flipped several times on the first leg and nearly drowned. "The third time they pulled us off the river. We were hypothermic and didn't even know it," Schnitzka says. "Sitting on the banks of the Rhine knowing basically that we were done ... crushed would be an understatement. We were devastated."

Perdzock retired after that, but Schnitzka was still determined to conquer the Rhine. The two had been racing partners since their first venture in 1982, a dare to paddle the 430-mile Wisconsin River.

Schnitzka started training with Hoffmann, nearly 25 years his junior, and the two set a record paddling across Lake Michigan last fall on a training run in 11 hours, 22 minutes. When they hit the Rhine next month, they are going to paddle for 21 hours a day, sleeping three in the canoe. "Once you hit the water it's 75 percent mental and 25 percent physical," Schnitzka says. "You can be amazed at what you can make your body do, but if you don't have a strong mind you will fail."

Preparing for the race — training, obtaining sponsorships, working out logistics — is nearly a full-time job. The trip covers seven countries with three different languages. "The rules and regulations in Europe are considerably different," Schnitzka says. A violation can lead to an arrest. And then there is the weather to contend with. "If Mother Nature throws too much at you, you will not break records. Period. That is the X factor that will make or break any of these events," Schnitzka says.

Besides the decades-old score to settle, Schnitzka says his motivation is simply to get as much out of life as he can. "This isn't a dress rehearsal for life," he says. "Why do people climb mountains? It's much more than that. You've pushed your body to the point of utter collapse and survived. How many people have ever done that?"

Schnitzka says he's very confident going into his last race before retiring. "I've logged more than 20,000 miles canoeing," he says. "There is nothing the Rhine has that I haven't done before."

27540513R00072

Made in the USA
Lexington, KY
05 January 2019